CHURCH WITHOUT WALLS

JIM PETERSEN

NAVPRESS

A MINISTRY OF THE NAVIGATORS
P.O.BOX 35001, COLORADO SPRINGS, COLORADO 80935

The Navigators is an international Christian organization. Jesus Christ gave His followers the Great Commission to go and make disciples (Matthew 28:19). The aim of The Navigators is to help fulfill that commission by multiplying laborers for Christ in every nation.

NavPress is the publishing ministry of The Navigators. NavPress publications are tools to help Christians grow. Although publications alone cannot make disciples or change lives, they can help believers learn biblical discipleship, and apply what they learn to their lives and ministries.

© 1992 by Jim Petersen
All rights reserved. No part of this publication may be reproduced in any form without written permission from NavPress, P.O. Box 35001, Colorado Springs, CO 80935.
Library of Congress Catalog Card Number: 91-67292
ISBN 08910-96639

Second printing, 1992

Cover illustration: Scott Snow

Printed in the United States of America

Contents

*To my many brothers and sisters in Christ
who long for greater participation
in God's purposes.*

Acknowledgments

▼

O ver the years my wife, Marge, has brought as much to our ministry as I have. Together we have lived the things I write about. But writing is a solitary effort. I know the months of concentration this manuscript has demanded of me have interrupted our normal pattern of colaboring together. But she never complained. She has only encouraged me.

I also want to thank Sue Gliebe, with whom I have worked these past sixteen years, for processing and reprocessing this manuscript until we felt we had it right. She, too, does it all with a wonderful spirit.

My friend and mentor, Jake Barnett, has been with me on this project since the beginning. I think it was in 1981 that we made the first outline for this book. He has helped me review and revise this manuscript line by line. Donald McGilchrist, Os Guinness, and Glenn McMahan have also helped greatly with their suggestions and contributions. Karen Hinckley, my editor, has been exceptional to work with. She has understood from the beginning what it is I am seeking to communicate with this manuscript, and has guided me toward my goal.

Foreword

▼

I n *Church Without Walls*, Jim Petersen—a veteran missionary
with The Navigators—wrestles with a very real global problem: how to reach an unbelieving world for Christ and at the
same time effectively build up the Body of Christ, enabling the
"church gathered" to be instructed, to worship, and to minister to
one another. Jim raises the issue—and rightly so—that both our
historical and present approaches to church structures reflect an
imbalanced preoccupation with gathering the church together to
care for itself. This preoccupation has tended to "program" out of
those structures the primary reason that Christ came into the
world: to seek and to save those who are lost. Jim contends
that, even since the early centuries, churches have neglected
to perpetuate the apostolic, "going" ministry introduced by Jesus
Christ and carried out by the first-century church.

This book will make church leaders all over the world uncomfortable with their present approaches to ministry. Using what he
believes are supracultural principles of Scripture, Jim challenges
our current ecclesiological structures. He argues for freedom in
form while holding tenaciously to New Testament functions.
Though some will question his rather broad approach to ecclesiology, none can question the importance and relevancy of the

9

biblical and cultural issues he addresses. Neither can anyone ignore the success Jim has experienced in applying these principles. He did this for over a quarter of a century in another culture of the world where people were basically secular and pagan. I have been there and seen it firsthand. He has earned the right to speak out in both the areas of evangelism and discipling Christians to reproduce themselves individually and corporately. Church leaders of all persuasions in all kinds of structures will do well to listen to what Jim writes in this book, to evaluate their own churches, and when necessary to make changes that will assist in being more effective in reaching an unbelieving world for Jesus Christ.

Dr. Gene A. Getz
Pastor, Fellowship Bible Church North
Director, Center for Church Renewal
Plano, Texas

Preface

▼

The thesis of this book developed while I was part of a two-couple team pioneering a ministry among young educated Brazilians. People were coming to faith who could not—and I had to admit, should not—embrace the church traditions that we represented. Identifying with our traditions confused them and isolated them from their peers, quenching the flow of the good news among them.

My personal doctrines of the church were proving to be inadequate for the situation. What was happening among those young Brazilians was obviously being done by God. I just could not fit it into what I believed concerning the church. I felt like the Apostle Peter in the house of Cornelius!

I was faced with a choice. I could abandon those people who refused to fit and go to a different class who were less sensitive to foreign forms, or I could continue with what I was doing and live with the tension of dealing with the obviously inevitable consequences. I recognized that there was really no choice, so with considerable apprehension I let go of my comfortable, familiar systems and let those young believers carry me into unknown territory.

Now in retrospect I realize that the most unbelievable part of the whole experience was the fact that I had any struggle at all. The years that followed were years of valuable learning from my friends and from our experiences in the light of the Scriptures. I soon realized that the limitations we were attempting to overcome were inherent in the church tradition of which I am a part. I believe the church at large lives with similar limitations. That realization is the motivation behind this book. The contents have gestated in my mind over the years. On several occasions I thought I was ready to put them down on paper, but I'm glad that I waited until now. I wasn't ready. I'm still not, but a sense of urgency over our present situation drives me. I hope I have come far enough in my thinking to engage you in the ideas that I raise in such a way that together we can do something about them.

I feel another hesitation as I write. My subject has to do with something that is very close to God's heart—people. On the day Christ died God showed us how He feels about people in general. The promises He makes to those who are His are beyond belief. I am on sacred ground, and I do not take that lightly. As I wrote this book I prayed that my words would encourage and clarify, that the reader would come away with a clear understanding of what he or she has in Christ, and of what this life is to be all about for us.

Some of what I say may produce controversy. That is not my desire. I have attempted to be honest and speak the truth as I am able to understand it.

International readers will notice that I am writing with U.S. culture primarily in mind. However, while I follow the story of the North American church from 1628 onward, many of the conclusions I draw are relevant to the Protestant churches of Europe, as well as to those in other countries founded by Protestant missionaries from the West. I hope that Americanisms won't prove to be a barrier for international readers.

I am greatly indebted to several writers from whom I have borrowed extensively. I have drawn repeatedly from Allan Bloom's _The Closing of the American Mind._ Paul Johnson's _A History of Christianity_ served as a resource, especially for chapters 2 and 5. In chapter 5 I have also relied on Kenneth Scott Latourette's _A History of Christianity._

This book is about the church. I have discovered that one of the challenges in writing a book on this subject is to achieve precision in the use of the word *church*. The common usage of *church* refers to Christians who are organized and share a common structure. This is sometimes limited to a local organization, sometimes expanded to include local groups combined into what we call a denomination. While I cannot agree that this is an adequate definition of the church, the usage has become so commonplace that it would be virtually impossible to use the word in any other way.

That means that I must not only articulate a new definition, but find a word that expresses its essential meaning. I believe that the *ecclesia* of the New Testament describes *God's people, indwelt by the Holy Spirit, who are being transformed and gifted for service among their brothers and sisters and the unbelieving world*. I will refer simply to *God's people*, using other appropriate synonyms as they fit the context.

I will be using the term *God's people* for biblical times, and also in reference to the broader definition that I am proposing. *Church* will be used to refer to the organized church from the times of the Church Fathers, when the definition began to change, until today and our contemporary understanding and usage of the term. There are times in the book when these usages converge, so the distinctions have not always been easy to maintain.

"God's people" will refer to His people as they are engaged in all of the dimensions of life, wherever they are in life, in the world, and in whatever form or whatever organization. I do not want to exclude the many groups of Christians who have specialized functions in the world and in the body, or the function of Christians in the world as they live their lives outside of the church structure.

The popular definition of church puts too many essential functions of the body outside of the definition, and therefore outside of the church. For example, if we were referring to the presence of Christians in the day-to-day activities of a neighborhood, it would be obvious that the *church* could not be there. Our limited definition of *church* puts those activities outside of the church, and I want to include them in it.

Indeed, one of the objectives of this book is to expand our

thinking concerning the church in this manner. I trust that by the end of the book you will agree that this expansion is justified.

In the final analysis I believe that the church, even as we have expanded the definition to "God's people," is still not an adequate description of everything God is doing. There is a larger reality that commands our attention—the Kingdom of God.

I find it strange that references to the Kingdom of God are so prominent in the New Testament and so rare today. The good news of the Kingdom is the message that Jesus brought.[1] It is the message that Jesus said would be "preached in the whole world as a testimony to all nations, and then the end will come."[2] It is the message proclaimed by the Apostle Paul to the Gentiles.[3] The gospel of the Kingdom is the "rock" on which Jesus said, "I will build my church."[4]

There are more references in the New Testament to the Kingdom of God or the Kingdom of Heaven than there are to church or churches. I'm not implying that the church is unimportant, simply that it is not all that there is—there is something greater. When the good news of the Kingdom is preached, the church happens. When we concentrate on building the church, we tend to reproduce our familiar forms.

To begin to talk about the Kingdom of God would be to begin another book. Perhaps someday we can do that. Our topic in this book is the people of God.

Part I
CONTEMPORARY SOCIETY AND BIBLICAL TRUTH

CHAPTER ONE

The Reshaping
of the American Way of Life

▼

In his book *Discovering the Future*, Joel Barker tells the story of the quartz watch. Before World War II the Swiss held as much as 90 percent of the watch market in the world. They still held over 60 percent of the market in the 1970s. By the early 1980s their market share was below 10 percent. From 1979 to 1982 employment in Swiss watchmaking was cut from sixty-five thousand to fifteen thousand. The main factor in this sudden collapse of a world industry was the invention of the quartz watch.

Ironically, it was the Swiss who invented the quartz watch. In 1967 the Swiss watch manufacturers' research arm, The Swiss Watch Federation Research Center at Neuchâtel, created the first prototype. They presented it to the Swiss manufacturers, and they weren't interested in it!

There is no public record of the manufacturers' response, but Barker quotes the January 14, 1980, issue of *Fortune* magazine explaining what happened.

> The main villain proved to be the inflexibility of Swiss watchmakers. They simply refused to adjust to one of the biggest technological changes in the history of time keeping, the development of the electronic watch . . . Swiss

companies were so tied to traditional technology that they couldn't—or wouldn't—see the opportunities offered by the electronic revolution.[1]

The Swiss watchmakers knew watches. Theirs were the best in the world. Watches have wheels, levers, gears, and springs. They go "tick." The quartz watch had none of these. The Swiss *could not* see its potential.

So the inventors took their discovery to an international trade fair. There, too, the watch companies ignored it. Two nonwatchmakers, Seiko and Texas Instruments, saw the potential. The rest is history.

The Swiss watchmakers viewed their profession through a certain *paradigm*. "A paradigm is a set of assumptions that provide a satisfactory rationale for all of the day to day tasks and research in a given field."[2] One's paradigm determines what one is able to see—or not see. The Swiss watchmakers lost their market because of what they knew, or thought they knew, about watches. It took people who were not in the watch business to see the potential of the new invention. This is often the case because of our normal reluctance to abandon the familiar. However, willingness to change is necessary before we can take on another paradigm.

This story of the quartz watch describes a relatively minor example of a paradigmatic change. Others, scattered across our history, have permanently altered the way most of humanity views the world and lives life. The lesson for us here is that we all view our worlds through a pair of glasses. We operate within a paradigm and plug everything we see into that framework for seeing the world. It's hard for us to conceive of the idea that a different set of glasses could give us a different perspective on virtually everything we see.

When we look at the church, we view it through a traditional paradigm. For example, we all know churches have sanctuaries, pulpits, pews, and a clergy. For us it is difficult to think of a church without any of these familiar components.

But what if, for some reason, it suddenly became impossible to have these things? Would the church cease, or could we change our paradigm and carry on? God's people started without any of these things, and did very well. And God's people in East Asia have functioned basically without any of these resources for the past forty years.

A Christian from East Asia tells the story from his viewpoint. In October 1949 the Communists took over the country. All foreign missionaries were expelled, and the national leaders they had trained were either imprisoned or killed. In 1957, those who had persisted in the faith were sent to prison camps. All the official churches were under government control and were closed from 1966 to 1976. The surviving Christians were forced to change their understanding of church to survive. Survive they did, growing from five million to an estimated fifty million in a period of forty years.[3]

Why, you ask, do we even bother to talk about such things? Communism appears to be dying, and threats of prohibitive persecution are not imminent in this country. We do just fine with sanctuaries, pulpits, and pews. So what's the point?

True, it was persecution that forced a paradigm shift in the understanding of church onto believers in East Asia. But there are other more subtle factors that can be calling on the American church to go from sanctuaries, pulpits, pews, and clergy to forms we have never really seriously considered. Let me tell of my own experience with paradigm change.

In 1963 my wife and I moved to Brazil to minister. Our understanding of what the church was all about was simplistic. To us the church was the sum total of all the local churches in the world that preached grace by faith. I saw myself as a part of a parachurch group—people who come alongside the church to help. So I understood my work to be to win the lost, establish them in the faith, teach them to do what I was doing with others, integrate them into the churches, and keep moving. Our contribution would be new fruit, which would provide additional leadership and energy for the established church. The Protestant church was about 5 percent of the population of Brazil at that time.

We were starting from scratch. We literally didn't know anybody in the whole country. So it was tempting for me to consider going to the church first. I could help mobilize that 5 percent, I rationalized. But then I had to admit how foolish that idea was. I had yet to even mobilize myself in that culture! I had nothing to offer the church but theory from a foreign country. So we decided to go directly to the 95 percent, learning from experience.

We faced many other decisions as we began. Which city should we go to? What kind of people should we begin with: families, young working people, military, or students? For various reasons we settled on university students.

These decisions brought us a great, unexpected benefit. Starting as we did with nonbelievers, our cultural adaptation was learned through the people we were attempting to reach. We learned to see Brazil through their eyes, rather than through eyes that had already acquired a religious tradition. It was a fresh look. The country had just gone through a revolution. The student environment was highly politicized, with the majority being oriented toward Marxism. Consequently they rejected the institutions of the culture, whether related to the government or to the church.

As we established our first relationships, we found people to be suspicious of anything structured; they even rejected books and any other printed material. So we discarded everything but our Bibles and simply invited our new friends to take a look at the Bible to see if it had anything to say to them. We let them know we understood and accepted their unbelief. Gradually people began coming to Christ.

Simultaneously I became involved with a pastor in the German-Lutheran Church in Brazil. At that time, European liberal theology controlled that church. Consequently the Bible and the identity of Christ were under question by many. Recognizing the spiritual vacuum created by liberal theology, the pastor asked me to help him. Since about three million people were nominally attached to that denomination, the situation proved to be very fruitful. Thousands responded as we clarified the gospel among these people. We discipled the converts and enabled them to pass it on.

Unintentionally we were giving birth to two movements, one among the unchurched, secularized Brazilian, the other among people already identified with the church. We referred to them as the "religious Christians" and the "nonreligious Christians."

Then the time came, we thought, to bring the two together. That was a disaster.

We planned a weekend retreat and invited about one hundred fifty people, some from each movement. At the end of the first day they retired to a nearby outdoor refreshment area. Two circles formed: the religious Christians in one, the nonreligious in the other. The first group sang choruses and hymns, while the second played samba and drank beer. Judgments flew in every direction! Neither group felt the other was worthy of citizenship in God's Kingdom.

As we pondered the situation we realized that the attempt to homogenize those people into a single pattern would change everyone's identity, and both groups would lose their communication with their unbelieving friends. One group couldn't get along without sanctuaries, pulpits, pews, and clergy. The other couldn't get along with them. We decided to continue to relate the two groups on the leadership level, but keep them separate on the grass-roots level. Thus we preserved the ongoing outreach of both groups. But there was still a problem.

My plan to bring the secularized converts into the existing church had just collapsed. There we were, with increasing numbers of very secular people coming to Christ, and they had no place to go. Culturally and socially they were in a different world. As they graduated from the universities, they scattered out across the country. We had no choice but to continue to meet the spiritual needs of those people as they sought to build their lives around God's Word. Over the next two decades we proceeded with Bible in hand to pick our way into the future, committed to preserving the integrity and dynamic of both movements.

During those years, as the movement spread into the other Latin American countries and as I became involved in those places as well, everything I thought I knew continued to be challenged. Every country was different enough that I had to admit that the specifics of the experiences I was having in Brazil were not transferable, even to a neighboring country. In fact, I've observed that when we would attempt to transfer the specifics, things that were expressions of freedom in one situation became legalisms when imposed in another. Those experiences have driven me to study the Bible and to study people. The compelling question has been, How should God's people be expressing themselves if they are to be fruitful in the almost infinite variations of culture and religious traditions that exist in the world? Our responsibility is not only to the other cultures of the world, but to the unreached majority of our own. This places a heavy responsibility upon God's people in America. To this point we have failed to assume it.

So, this book is motivated by what I see in the American culture and in the American church. Much is being said and written about the enormous changes that the American society is undergoing. I believe these changes are self-evident. Our society is undergoing several paradigmatic changes simultaneously, but I don't see the church responding accordingly. We are making many cosmetic changes, but our basic perceptions remain unaltered. We continue to think "sanctuaries, pulpits, pews and clergy." These will undoubtedly continue to serve those of us who have a church heritage, and a certain number of those who do not. But we haven't asked what it will take to make the gospel truly accessible and transforming to the rest of this society. Do we have the creativity to assess the true needs, and the mobility to go into our world in an effectual manner?

SIX INFLUENCES CURRENTLY SHAPING AMERICA

The following paragraphs are a sample of some of the influences that are bringing about major changes in this country, and that will undoubtedly greatly influence the church in one way or another. There are other influences of importance, but the six I have chosen to address are among the most basic. They are affecting us all regardless of our race, employment, financial situation, or place of residence.

Our View of Truth Is Becoming Increasingly Relativistic
Perhaps the most significant trend in America is the change taking place in our view of truth. Allan Bloom has been a professor of social thought for over forty years. He begins his book *The Closing of the American Mind* with the following sentence: "There is one thing a professor can be absolutely certain of: almost every

student entering the university believes, or says he believes, that truth is relative. . . . The relativity of truth is not a theoretical insight but a moral postulate."[4]

Bloom's thesis is that if we cannot accept anything as true, we cannot really think at all. We cannot make progress in our reasoning. It also follows that this relativism makes it very difficult for the individual to make it through life without a serious crash or two along the way. That is because words like "right and wrong" and "moral and immoral" lose all real meaning. "Good" is what one finds rewarding. Robert Bellah describes this in *Habits of the Heart*: "If one's preferences change, so does the nature of the good. Even the deepest ethical virtues are justified as matters of personal preference. Indeed, the ultimate ethical rule is simply that individuals should be able to pursue whatever they find rewarding."[5] There are only two constraints: don't impose your ideas on the person next to you, and don't harm Mother Nature.

So an individual will embark on a lifestyle based on an ad hoc collection of values gathered from parents, the media, a favorite professor, a movie, or whatever. He or she embarks into life—and things begin to fall apart. After a pause to collect some new values, the person tries again. Mercifully, life is short enough to allow time for only a limited number of such crashes. What is missing is an undergirding body of truth.

In spite of the fact that relativism cannot be lived without inflicting a great deal of pain, it is rapidly becoming the prevailing ideology of our society.

Long-range Prospects of Scarcity and Downward Mobility

The 1983 National Commission of Excellence in Education cited one analyst assaying, "For the first time in the history of our country, the educational skills of one generation will not surpass, will not equal, will not even approach, those of their parents."[6] Recent trends indicate that each year the typical American child is increasingly likely to be born in poverty and to grow up in a broken family. But even many of those from stable families and with college educations face the prospect of diminishing financial returns. The deterioration of our educational systems combined with job scarcity and underemployment are changing prospects for the future. "Sociologists call the predicament down-ward mobility. They mean simply that young adults will not have the income or the status that their parents had. They will almost certainly not enjoy the life-style."[7]

When we balance this projection of diminishing abilities against our overwhelming multitrillion-dollar federal debts, it is hard not to conclude that the affluence so many of us now take for granted could easily come to an end.

Time Becomes a Most Precious Commodity

Time magazine ran a cover story titled "How America Has Run Out of Time." In essence, the article reported that the technology that produced the information revolution has not delivered the leisure lifestyle it advertised. To the contrary, we are discovering that our time and labor-saving devices just speed everything up. We simply fill the time we gain with more work. Our machines run us. We have phones in our cars, we carry laptops when we board a plane, and the fax machine makes it all happen now.

But technology is not the sole culprit. The article went on to say the time famine we are experiencing is also a consequence of our economic expectations. Families find it takes two paychecks to fund the middle-class way of life. "The increasing rarity of the full-time homemaker has done more to eat away everyone's leisure time than any other factor. . . . Single-parent households are squeezed even more."[8] Grade-school children find themselves pressed into doing adult duties as they too get caught in the rush.

This drive to maintain the middle-class way of life is not the whole story, as the article would lead us to think. When the income tax was introduced, the rate was 0.5 percent. You are familiar with the rates we pay today. High taxes, costly insurance rates, and the soaring costs of education converge to put this generation under pressure.

Americans have had to trade time for money. This leaves them without time to relax and to parent their children. Pollster Lou Harris is quoted as saying, "Time . . . may have become the most precious commodity in the land."[9] The irony of it is that this trade hasn't worked. Economist Robert J. Shapiro reports that "from

1970 to 1990, despite an increase to 51 percent from 29 percent in the number of mothers in the work force who have children under age 5, the mean income of families with young children remained stagnant."[10]

The Pursuit of Self-Fulfillment
Wanda Urbanska, representing her generation of twenty-year-olds during the 1980s, writes, "We are a generation raised on Jack-in-the-Box hamburgers and Diet Pepsi, not home cooking and whole milk. Without anything about which to feel secure, the singular generation . . . never learned how to trust—in love, in marriage, in children and even in the religious and secular institutions in which our predecessors once laid their faith." Instead, she goes on to say, "We have narrowed our scope of vision to the small picture—our lives, our homes, our careers, our bodies and our hobbies. We are tense, intense, mistrustful, perpetually ill at ease. . . . more attuned to the devastation of divorce than the security of marriage."[11]

This retreat into absorption with self is not so much narcissism (self-admiration and the need to be admired) as it is an expression of disillusionment with anything larger than one's private world. This generation has been let down over and over again. In the past twenty years we have suffered the greatest political scandal in the nation's history. We have gone through deep economic crises. Religious leaders have discredited the religious institutions. Our teachers failed to educate us. And mom and dad are off somewhere on their own pursuits. It is no wonder this generation has turned inward.

The price they are paying is the inability to establish and maintain enduring relationships, whether in marriage, with their families, or with friends.

The Redefining of the Family
It was "feminism that sent women back to the job market—even if it was the economy that kept them there."[12] For many women, being a wife and mother is no longer an acceptable way of life.

"Women want financial independence and achievement apart from their families, and this means that their mothers probably won't serve as role models. It is also a problem that affects young men. If women won't be homemakers, men don't have to be providers, and they too are cut loose to explore other definitions of themselves."[13] This redefinition of roles, of what it means to be a woman or a man, could become one of the most crucial social issues of the 1990s.

The victims in this redefinition are the children. Judith Mack, the director of counseling at the University of California, Davis, says her department's most difficult therapy-resistant cases come from homes where parents were so caught up in the momentum of their own lives that they hardly had time to be functioning parents. Their children were given every advantage, including continuous therapy, but what they needed were parents. "Kids like this just haven't the emotional resources to handle even campus life on their own," Mack states.[14]

The shortage of time is a significant element here. "The transfer of time from the home to the workplace has been massive," says social historian Barbara Whitehead. She cites studies that show parents today spend 40 percent less time with their children than parents of a generation ago, a statistic that

> represents a significant social disinvestment in our children. It's not just that mothers walk around in a perpetual fog of fatigue. Time has a cultural meaning. Although we have one-minute managers, there is no such thing as a one-minute parent.
>
> If parents are not around to influence the values of kids, other forces move in—drugs, TV, the mall, peers.[15]

Increase in Personally and Socially Destructive Behavior

Last year Chuck Wenger, who was then the director of Sports World Ministries, sought my involvement in their ministry to high school students. He showed me a stack of cards they had gathered from students from across the nation. The problems the kids wrote about on those cards revolved repeatedly around three themes: drugs, sexual abuse, and suicide. I am told responses demonstrate few differences between suburban schools and inner-city schools.

The drug epidemic is a part of the legacy we received from the 1960s. Drug use was the hip vice of jazz musicians and other artists. Now it has become a disease that threatens the nation. Crime and violence are inevitable fellow travelers with drug trade and usage. Newscasters reported there were 25,000 murders in the United States in 1990. We live in fear. We triple bolt our doors and worry about our children while they play in the neighborhood park. Why are our kids so vulnerable to the neighborhood junkie? As we look at the society we've been describing here, this destructive behavior becomes understandable.

I could describe other major forces contributing to social change, such as the information revolution, urbanization, the recomposition of the nation's ethnic mix, or the implications of the baby boom. But what we have here is sufficient to make our point. One way of life appears to be ending, and another is emerging.

ENTER THE PEOPLE OF GOD

As we reflect upon these trends we come away with a picture of a nation in trouble, struggling with a potentially lethal mix of forces. This mix has already claimed millions of victims—people whose private worlds have been broken in one way or another. This society hurts.

Christians have dual citizenship, in God's Kingdom and in this nation in which we live. The inescapable question becomes, What is our responsibility here? The world is broken for us as well, and often coping with our own pain seems to be more than we can handle. Yet God calls on us to go beyond ourselves. He has purposely placed us in this world as salt, light, and good seed. Jesus prayed to His Father, "As you have sent me into the world, I have sent them into the world."[16] God's people are sent to cure, to enlighten, and to offer life. But how do we do that? To date, the solutions we have offered have been superficial and piecemeal.

We tend to lay our hands on whatever looks like it might help. For example, we have learned to utilize technology. The church has become skilled in media use, generating and moving information as deftly as anyone in the marketplace. This can be beneficial, but it has allowed us to slip into the notion that information dissemination *is* the ministry. If we can just get information out, we've done our job.

Another tendency is to think that additional personnel will be our solution. When confronted with a need, we tend to hire another pastor "to get something going in that area," and from then on it's his problem. We seem to think we can take care of any problem with personnel.

This book is about God's people in the world. It is an attempt to call us away from the pragmatism that says, "We're okay as long as our numbers are up." It is a call to take a serious look at a changing world that is suffering profound, agonizing needs. It is a call for us to make a break with the inertia of our past and to return to the Scriptures for a fresh look at what it says God's people should be and do in times like these. I submit these thoughts to you with the prayer that God will lead us together into a more complete understanding of His will in the matters under discussion, and then on into doing His work in His way.

CHAPTER TWO

Our Contemporary Society: Where We Got It and Where It Is Going

▼

The trends I have just described are not merely one more passing summer storm. They have the momentum of centuries of history behind them and have already found their way into our neighborhoods. The person next door or across the way has a worldview that is truly different from ours as Christians.

A few years ago our family moved from Brazil back to the United States. This country had become a foreign place to us during the years we had been away, especially for our children. None of us really knew what to expect. We had kept abreast of the trends, but we had not experienced living with them. We were aware that the country's heritage of biblical religion was eroding, but we were also aware that the United States continued to serve as the matrix of the modern missionary movement, that it continued to be a country filled with vigorous churches.

The city we were moving to epitomized the strengths of the evangelical church. Although the city is not large, it contains a number of outstanding churches and also serves as home base for over a dozen major Christian organizations. Certainly there at least, we thought, the Christian presence would still prevail. As we made our way out of Brazil, I remember wondering about our future neighbors. I assumed that many of them would already be Christians. As we settled into our new surroundings over the next months, we set out to get to know our neighbors. As our new circle of acquaintances grew and as friendships developed, we became aware of the pain that seemed to be everywhere. There was the man who lived alone except for occasional weekends when his three small children came to visit. Several times new families would scarcely settle into a house before a for-sale sign would appear on the front lawn. The couple was splitting up.

We saw more of the same as our children began bringing their new school friends around. I will never forget the day our twin nineteen-year-old daughters brought twenty of their schoolmates over to celebrate the completion of their first year in college. We conversed for hours and enjoyed them immensely. But it didn't take long to realize that virtually all of those young people were struggling with serious personal crises. Most of them were alienated from parents, who more often than not had separated. Most of them used drugs; some had attempted suicide. One young man in a long ponytail was so glassy-eyed he probably didn't really see anything or anybody that afternoon.

People in this society do many self-destructive things. They repeatedly make choices that set them up for inevitably painful consequences. But what they *do* isn't as frightening as is the way they *think*. One backyard conversation with a neighbor serves to illustrate how many people think today.

Our discussion was moving toward spiritual issues, and at one point I said, "If we are going to think together, we need at least to understand how the other views truth. Can we agree that, somewhere, truth exists?" I was fully expecting an affirmative answer when my neighbor shot back, "Of course not!" His response startled me. It was automatic, like a recitation from a different catechism. To him relativism was a given, and my belief that truth is knowable had caught him by surprise.

As our family worked its way through these adjustments, I found that at times I was responding with anger! I was angry at the parents and at this society that is passing on such a miserably bankrupt heritage to our next generation. I was angry with the Christian community. Surely, I thought, the influence of the many churches and Christian organizations should have been far greater in this city. Except for one Mormon family and another that practices Christian Science, no one in our new neighborhood attends church. The others have no interest, and the way things are they never will. Given their assumptions, seeking out a church is about the last thing they would think of doing. Jesus described our neighborhood when He observed that the people in the villages He visited were "harassed and helpless, like sheep without a shepherd." This description of His is apt for the rest of the nation as well.

We live in a society that is in great pain. How can it be that this wealthy, richly gifted church of ours can coexist alongside of it and demonstrate so little redemptive influence? What happened to the spiritual heritage that was passed on to this nation? Where and how did we lose it?

What did happen? The answer is a long story, but it is an important one for us to know and understand. History is not a popular subject these days—it seems so much less relevant than the evening news. Surprisingly, history can sometimes tell us more about the present than the current issue of *Time.* In this chapter we will take a brief excursion into the past for the purpose of helping us understand the present.

In a later chapter we will take a second, more comprehensive trip through history. But then we will be watching for something different. For now, we are seeking to understand the forces that created our present spiritual climate.

We will begin in the fourth century with Augustine. (Trust me, Augustine really is relevant to modern America.) We will divide the interval between his time and ours into three parts: Augustine and the Middle Ages, the period of the Enlightenment, and modern times.

Once again I want to acknowledge my heavy reliance on three sources for much of the factual material in this chapter as well as chapter 5: *A History of Christianity,* by Kenneth Scott Latourette; Paul Johnson's book of the same title; and Johnson's *Modern Times.* I have, of course, acknowledged direct quotations from these books in the footnotes, but in addition have utilized a great deal of material from them. These two authors' writings have made such a contribution to my knowledge of history that I often find myself expressing things using their terminology.

AUGUSTINE OF HIPPO (AD 354–431) AND THE MIDDLE AGES

"No other Christian after Paul was to have so wide, deep, and prolonged an influence upon the Christianity of Western Europe . . . as had Augustine."[1] For over a thousand years, Augustine remained the most popular of the Church Fathers. His *Confessions*, written in AD 397, are still read today, probably because the book, autobiographical in nature, describes a young, sinful Augustine striving to overcome his sexual impulses. Apparently, this is a timeless problem. His most important book, *City of God*, changed the Western world for over a millennium. We still struggle with its central concept, the ideal of a totally Christian society. Such a society is necessarily compulsory, requiring the unification of church and state and the use of force to maintain religious conformity. Augustine interpreted the phrase "compel them to come in" from Luke 14:23 as a justification for the infliction of physical pain for the sake of gaining religious unity.[2] Teaching, he said, "can be done with the greatest ease when the teaching of truth is aided by the fear of severity."[3] The empire applied this principle in the persecution of the Donatists, probably with more brutality than Augustine had envisioned. The basic concept of church and crown working together generated new applications throughout the Dark Ages, eventually serving as the doctrinal basis for the terrors of the Inquisition.

Augustine helped lay the foundations for the medieval church, which assumed the responsibility to legislate every aspect of conduct, to bring the actual behavior of individuals into line with Christian teaching—and to call on the state to enforce that legislation. Membership in society was gained by baptism into the Church. Baptism was compulsory and irrevocable. Those who violated their baptism by infidelity or heresy faced death.

But there was also much good. "In the Dark Ages, the Church had stood for everything that was progressive, enlightened and humane in Europe."[4] Also, primarily through the monastic orders the countryside was tamed and made productive for agriculture. Thus the church contributed greatly to the spiritual and material wealth of the continent. For centuries the church was regarded with affection and respect because of its benign influence.

However, a person living in the Middle Ages could only look at life in one way—through the view taught by the clergy. This view was pessimistic in the sense that it was excessively other-worldly. Eternal salvation was the foremost preoccupation and was a costly, uncertain affair. Earthly life, by contrast, was viewed as being quite pointless.

Predictably, the applications of Augustine's concept of a "city of God" caused frequent tensions between the church and the crown. The state without the church was nothing, and the church couldn't get along without the state. At times the state had the supremacy; at other times it was the pope. Gradually, this interfacing with the state turned the church into a totally different kind of institution. "It became not so much a divine society, as a legal one."[5] As the church became increasingly involved in legal matters, conflict with the state increased accordingly. By the beginning of the fifteenth century, the image of the church was financial and political, not spiritual—a perfect climate for corruption.

The business of salvation became the sale of relics, indulgences, special privileges, masses for the dead. This began to produce fundamental changes in attitude toward the church. People began to view the clergy with disfavor, feeling they abused their privileges and were coercive.

Because of this perceived corruption, the church began to lose its hold on the populace. It committed two other offenses that were costly to its authority, especially with the intellectuals of the day. The first of these was the horrific tortures and executions the church meted out with regularity to people over even minor differences in points of doctrine. The second was its dogmatic rejection of scientific thought. One example of the latter was the harsh treatment of Galileo by the Roman Inquisition in 1633 because of his exposition of Copernican theory. These failings caused reactions that energized the Enlightenment.

Since our purpose in this chapter is to identify the primary origins of contemporary thought, we will step across the Reformation for now, and go directly to the Enlightenment, which was a reaction against the unreformed church.

THE ENLIGHTENMENT: AGE OF REASON (1600–late 1700s)

A succession of thinkers led Western society out of the religiously oriented worldview of the Middle Ages into one where human reason was central. Copernicus and Galileo were the early forerunners of this movement, which eventually came to be known as the Enlightenment, or Age of Reason.

The Enlightenment was energized by the birth of natural science through men such as Francis Bacon, Sir Isaac Newton, René Descartes, and John Locke. Bacon (1561–1626) and Descartes (1596–1650) developed the theories that allowed nature to be independently studied. Bacon's basic theme was the developing of a system of knowledge that would give man power over his environment. Building on this, René Descartes saw the possibilities of scientific reductionism—that nature can be reduced to its components, which can then be studied independently.

Newton provided the idea of establishing empirical proof for such studies. He and his colleagues did not foresee the conflict that has since arisen between our understanding of God and science. Instead they believed that knowledge was indivisible, that knowledge of the supernatural and of the natural world were inextricably linked. Science would confirm religious truth.

While these scientists themselves were sincere Christians, they realized that "institutional Christianity, with its feuds and intolerances, was an embarrassment and a barrier to scientific endeavor."[6] Enlightenment scientists finally concluded that they could not progress in their exploration of the natural world if they admitted matters of religion into their discussions. So they ruled them out. The why questions—the questions of origins—were banished from the laboratories.

John Locke (1623–1704) accepted the existence of God and the fact that Jesus is the Son of God as a "plain, intelligible proposition."[7] In his book *The Reasonableness of Christianity*, he developed the idea that Christianity ought to be subjected to the same rigorous tests as any scientific proposition. But Locke, with this thesis, provided the essential idea that later produced the divorce between religion and politics.

In effect, Locke removed God from man's everyday affairs. He envisioned an uninvolved God who left it up to man to use his power over nature and to produce; he maintained that meaning and purpose are found in productivity and consumption. He believed self-interest would be an adequate motivating force to supply civil society with all it needed and wanted.

Natural science came to be perceived by the intelligentsia as the emancipator from the superstitions and prejudices that prevailed throughout the religious institutions. Reason promised to offer liberation. Meanwhile, the Roman Catholic Church continued to fuel this pursuit of freedom and to further undermine their waning influence by persisting in committing atrocities. For example, in 1766 a young man, Chevalier de la Barre, failed to take off his hat while a religious procession passed through the streets. (It was raining.) "He was charged and convicted of blasphemy, and sentenced to 'the torture ordinary and extraordinary', his hands to be cut off, his tongue torn out with pincers and to be burned alive."[8]

These kinds of horrors prompted Voltaire (1694–1778) to write to Frederick the Great, "Your Majesty will do the human race an eternal service in extirpating this infamous superstition, I do not say among the rabble, who are not worthy of being enlightened and who are apt for every yoke; I say among the well-bred, among those who wish to think."[9]

Allan Bloom outlines three challenges to the rationalism of the Enlightenment—by Rousseau, Machiavelli, and Nietzsche.[10]

Rousseau was the first to "rain on the party." He agreed with Locke that man created his own society by contract, for the sake of self-preservation, but he further maintained that people have primitive feelings, sentiments that come from nature itself that make reason alone an inadequate mechanism for the establishing of society. Rousseau's arguments for this opposition between nature and society were so persuasive that they destroyed the self-confidence of the Enlightenment.

Machiavelli went further. He held that people have desires

that, whatever they might be, should be listened to. He asserted that our desires become the criteria for right and wrong, and they should have the last word as to how we live.

Friedrich Nietzsche (1844–1900) spent the greater part of his life studying religion in the belief that religion is the most important human phenomenon in understanding man. He saw the contradictions within Enlightenment thought and concluded that rationalism is inadequate, that it cannot be defended logically, and that it bore intolerable social consequences. Man longs to believe, he maintained, but God is dead, killed by the Enlightenment. Since there is nothing to believe in, man must muster the courage to press on in the face of the abyss of atheism.

Thus the Enlightenment completed a divorce between religion and science. This reinforced the break between religion and state.

MODERN TIMES (late 1700s–present)

Paul Johnson begins his book *Modern Times* by crediting three people with setting the stage for the present. They are Albert Einstein (1879–1955), Karl Marx (1818–83), and Sigmund Freud (1856–1939). This is perhaps an oversimplification, but it is true that each did profoundly influence modern thought. All three were products of the Enlightenment. All operated under the umbrella of the works of Charles Darwin (1809-1892).[11]

Darwin's *Origin of the Species*, in which he expounds his theories of evolution, natural selection, and social determinism, gave people what they were looking for: an alternative explanation for how the natural world came to exist. Without such a theory, atheism was untenable. It was virtually nonexistent in the Middle Ages. But in Darwin people finally had a rational case for their unbelief. The exodus from the church that had begun in the early 1800s was greatly accelerated in the 1850s and 1860s under the impact of Darwin's teachings.

In 1905, Albert Einstein published a paper, "On the Electrodynamics of Moving Bodies." Later his thesis became known as the Special Theory of Relativity. His discovery that space and time are relative rather than absolute terms, and his demonstration in 1907 that all mass has energy, provided a comprehensive revision of Newtonian physics. Einstein's careful, scientifically rigorous work was misinterpreted by the public. When "it was grasped that absolute time and absolute length had been dethroned . . . the belief began to circulate, for the first time at a popular level, that there were no longer any absolutes: of time and space, of good and evil, of knowledge, above all of value. Mistakenly but perhaps inevitably, relativity became confused with relativism."[12]

At about the same time, Freudianism came into public attention. Freud contributed to the message that the world was not what it seemed. His thesis was that neuroses were the result of the suppression of our natural, primitive instincts, that the personal conscience was something created by society to protect civilized order, and that personal feelings of guilt were a harmful illusion. He coined terms such as the *unconscious*, the *ego*, the *id*, the *superego, sublimation, guilt complex, death instinct*, etc., to communicate the idea that man is constantly, subconsciously, working at remolding reality. He dismissed religion as being "illusions, fulfillments of the oldest, strongest, and most insistent wishes of mankind."[13]

Karl Marx added another dimension to relativistic thinking. He wrote, "The final pattern of economic relationships as seen on the surface . . . is very different from, and indeed quite the reverse of, their inner but concealed essential pattern."[14] He theorized that economic forces were irresistible and will eventually have their way just as a great river will inevitably cut its own course. Our efforts at altering that course by exerting our wills and by taking measures to the contrary are ultimately futile.

The combined effect of Darwin, Einstein, Freud, and Marx undermined the sense of personal responsibility and of duty. Since nothing is as it appears to be, the individual can only conclude that something or someone else is responsible for what is going on. The result of this was moral anarchy.

In summary, the God-oriented worldview of the Middle Ages was replaced with one centered around human reason. But we've also seen how it didn't take long for people to realize that the human mind is inadequate for the task of constructing a rational, comprehensive worldview. Thus the conclusion: Since human reason is inadequate, truth is beyond our grasp. Ergo, truth becomes relative. These conclusions, however, were ignored, and society proceeded as if the human mind was, in fact, adequate.

This progression of thought helped spawn the two world wars and modernity. Our excursion into the past would be seriously lacking if we did not take a look at both of these.

THE WORLD WARS

It was hard for European Christians not to feel that their religion let them down during the world wars, at the time when they needed it the most. It was one country with its state church against another. European Christianity, supposedly based on a common moral foundation, proved impotent at its moment of truth. For centuries, the church had intensely debated and defended major and minor differences in doctrine, but World War I demonstrated the irrelevance of this effort. It was Christian killing Christian, with each believing God was on his side.

World War II further devastated the church's self-esteem. There are notable examples of Christians who courageously stood against Hitler and his regime. Many were imprisoned. Some died. Dietrich Bonhoeffer is a well-known example. In 1934 the Barmen Declaration was drafted by Christians to repudiate the Nazi regime.

By and large, however, the church capitulated to Hitler. Rome signed a concordat with him in 1933. The Lutherans collaborated, some groups even looking upon Hitler's movement as "saviors."[15]

Hitler scorned this cowering response from the religious leaders. He said, "Do you really believe the masses will ever be Christian again? Nonsense. Never again. . . . The parsons . . . will betray their God to us. They will betray anything for the sake of their miserable little jobs and incomes."[16]

In many ways the wars demonstrated the weakness of the churches. The wars embarrassed them. Their embarrassment is not unlike some of the feelings we Americans demonstrate in relation to some aspects of the Viet Nam conflict. Surely there must be a cause and effect between the behavior of the church in the two world wars and the present spiritual climate of Western

Europe. The countries of France, Germany, and those to the north of them can only be described as "cold." Many churches in that part of the world are little more than museums to a period in history of past spiritual vigor.

MODERNITY

The term *modernization* was coined to refer to the effects of the scientific process on modern civilization. The scientific process brought on revolutions in economics, industry, technology, and politics. It has transformed human life around the globe.[17]

Os Guinness describes modernity as a way of thinking that grows out of living in a society characterized by institutions, bureaucracies, technologies, urbanization, mass media, global economics, etc.[18] It imposes *rationalization*, the belief that the use of the human mind—knowledge—is the key to advancement of humanity. Rationalization transforms us into data, feasibility-study, and research junkies. If something can't be measured or quantified, we hardly know how to deal with it. It also imposes *privatization*: the cleavage between public and private spheres of a person's life. Privatization restricts one's spiritual life to the home and the church. It makes a virtue out of saying, "My religion is personal; I don't like to talk about it." Faith becomes irrelevant to daily life with privatization. Modernity also imposes *pluralization*, which makes all manner of worldviews, faiths, and ideologies acceptable. It consequently lowers one's commitment to any particular choice. It says, "I'll give this group a try; if it doesn't work out, I'll try another." So we change jobs, cars, spouses, values, and doctrines with ease.

The net effect of modernity on the church can hardly be overstated. Guinness graphically describes this in quoting Peter Berger: "The Christian Church contributed to the rise of the modern world; the modern world, in turn, has undermined the Christian Church. Thus, to the degree that the Church enters, engages and employs the modern world uncritically, the Church becomes her own gravedigger."[19]

Modernity causes the church to buy into the business model for doing its work and defining its success. It causes it to soften its claims that "truth lies here," and it leaves the individual believer with a compartmentalized faith that scarcely makes any difference at home, in the marketplace, or even in the inner life. Perhaps herein lies the answer to the question raised at the beginning of this chapter: What happened to our spiritual heritage? As we Christians have absorbed the modern mind-set, we have lost faith in the power of the truths we profess to believe. This has so diluted our convictions that they no longer really make much difference at all.

LOOK WHAT'S COMING!

As the Enlightenment dawned on the Western world, it was received as a reprieve from a repressive, dogmatic religious system. But as we saw, that sense of freedom was short-lived. Rousseau demonstrated that people have yearnings that Locke's one-dimensional message of work in the pursuit of self-interest didn't satisfy. Then Nietzsche argued that we cannot live without religion, that people long to believe, but that unfortunately there was nothing out there to believe in. In spite of these arguments to the effect that human reason is an untrustworthy guide, we embraced it. Both good and bad have grown out of the Enlightenment. We have seen the human mind produce an array of brilliant works of art, scientific discoveries, and technological advancements. But it has also brought the horrors of totalitarianism and refinements in the perverse art of war. These influences have propelled the Western world into a rapid, uninterrupted slide away from God into secularization, particularly since World War II.

To be secularized is to live without God in one's frame of reference. The biblical synonym is *ungodliness*. It means getting up in the morning, eating breakfast, going to work, returning home, watching the news, and going to bed at night—without involving God in those affairs. It is, simply, living without God. The problem with secularization is that it, like Marxism, is too meager a diet for the human soul. People can only live like that so long before they yearn for something more. Then they will either make a golden calf, worship something else of their own making, or pray to the stars. That, I believe, is where Western society is currently heading.

In the Enlightenment, man replaced God as the center of the Western worldview. Today nature has begun to replace man. There are a number of signs indicating that this is the direction society is headed as it searches to satisfy its spiritual yearnings. As always, with any new trend, there is much that is good in what is going on. This trend comes as a response to true needs that are really critical. Just as the Enlightenment emerged as a reaction against the repressive environment of the religious institutions of the Middle Ages, this trend comes as we awaken to the mess we've made of our planet. We have finally begun to realize that we cannot continue our wanton abuse of nature. We have a long way to go, but we are beginning to clean things up. This newfound concern for nature is a cause for celebration. But falsehood often grows out of carrying a truth too far—to its illogical conclusion.

There are a number of indications that this is what we are doing. As ecology becomes an increasingly important part of our lives, our view of nature is affected. A friend of mine, a department head at a state university in a field of natural science, said, "I constantly run into the deification of nature among my students. 'Mother Earth' has become their new goddess." This deification of nature results in a serious, dangerous error, as it confuses the line God draws between man and the rest of His creation. I suspect that many of the crusades for animal rights—the demonstrations against using animals in medical research, the opposition against using fur and leather, etc.—are prompted by this kind of confusion. According to the Bible, man alone is made in God's image. Creation is for man, but he is to be responsible and humane in his use of it. In Genesis 9:3-6, God says,

> Everything that lives and moves will be food for you. Just as I give you the green plants, I now give you everything.
>
> But you must not eat meat that has its lifeblood still in it. And for your lifeblood I will surely demand an accounting. I will demand an accounting from every animal. And from each man, too, I will demand an accounting for the life of his fellow man.
>
> Whoever sheds the blood of man,

by man shall his blood be shed;
for in the image of God
has God made man.

To depart from God's order by ignoring the line between human life and natural life is to degrade man. It does not elevate natural life as some may think, but it lowers human life to where it loses the unique value assigned to it by God. Any philosophy, or worldview, that has a flawed understanding of human nature is dangerous. That is the primary flaw in Marxism, where man is seen as a product of the evolutionary process. Combining evolution with Marx's dialectical view of history, people could only view themselves as being objects, hopelessly adrift like flotsam on the stream of history. The individual is expendable to the achieving of the collective "good." It took seventy years and scores of millions of lives to prove Marx wrong. This new trend also has the potential for that kind of evil.

NEW AGE

The New Age Movement embodies the trends I have been describing. This movement is difficult to describe, as it does not have an organized set of beliefs. Yet, as a movement, it is organized. It is becoming an eclectic world religion that resembles Eastern religious systems, rather than biblical religion. Its major premise is that all is one: nature is God, man is nature, therefore man is God. Nature becomes the center by which humans find their meaning. Its basic message is that you create your own reality. It is a close relative to Hinduism.

As New Age beliefs elevate nature, they accordingly devalue human life. Suddenly people find their lives have no priority over any other form of life. Belief in reincarnation helps to further justify this position. Murderous acts make no difference since, for example, an aborted fetus can find his soul in another fetus or possibly in an animal. This sinister thinking will quickly lead to corresponding behavior.

The ideas of the New Age Movement are now pervasive in American culture. It has major influence on science, education, politics, art, and the media. The ultimate objective of the movement is to create a new political set of values and standards, to shape a new global political and social vision.

New Age is especially attractive to America's unchurched generation. Many are finding they cannot live on secularization and have begun to search for a religious experience that neither established religions nor science has been able to provide. In New Age, people find a medium through which they can perform religious rituals such as chanting, yoga, and meditations, but that leaves the self and its natural desires unchecked. It has been described as a form of hyperselfism.[20]

Summary
What we have said can be summarized with the following diagram:

THREE SUCCESSIVE WORLD VIEWS

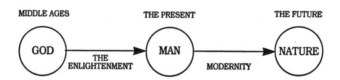

The God-oriented worldview of the Middle Ages was replaced by a man-centered worldview. The Enlightenment, or Age of Reason, was a transitional force in that change. The economic and industrial revolutions begat modernity, the way of thinking that comes from living in an institutional, technological world. Modernity creates a spiritual famine. It is my opinion that many will attempt to satisfy this hunger by making nature the new center of their worldview. We are becoming postmodern. In chapter 10 we will pick up on this discussion and take it further.

FIVE HUNDRED YEARS IN FIFTEEN VERSES

There is a striking parallel between the sequence of this five-hundred-year process and Romans 1:18-32. This passage describes the process by which a society moves away from God, into judgment. The value of this passage to this discussion is that it not only gives God's perspective on what has happened around us, it explains why it happened. It also tells us where the solution lies. It would require an extra chapter to do a worthy exposition of these fifteen verses. I will limit my comments here to a quick overview.

The passage breaks the process down into four stages, each culminating in a fall. The first is a stage of *God-consciousness*. In this phase the self-evident truths about God—that He is all-powerful, consciously purposeful, and holy—are acknowledged. The first steps away from God are in the direction of self-aggrandizement. They consist of failing to give God His rightful, central position in our lives and of not giving thanks. To give thanks is to acknowledge the giver, while unthankfulness is an expression of self-centeredness. As the Middle Ages gave way to the Age of Reason, the religious institutions served, overwhelmingly, to glorify man rather than God. This led to the first of four "falls" found in this passage.

Spiritual Fall

It could be called a *spiritual fall*, away from God into *confidence in self*. The passage reads, "Although they knew God . . . their thinking became futile and their foolish hearts were darkened. Although they claimed to be wise, they became fools." It would be difficult to coin a more apt description of the Enlightenment as a rejection of God as our premise for the sake of embracing human reason. We took this step even while we acknowledged the inadequacy of reason as a guide. This led to the second fall.

Intellectual Fall

When man embraced reason as his guide, he, in effect, threw away his compass. He rejected God as his point of reference and plunged himself into confusion. Under those conditions anything can happen. The passage reads, "They exchanged the truth of God for a lie, and worshiped and served created things rather than the Creator." In the confusion, we became a society of idolaters, worshiping technology, possessions, power, our children, sports, the institutions of our own making, birds, animals, reptiles—and on and on. With our affections thus misplaced, the third fall became predictable.

Moral Fall

The passage describes this third fall as follows: "Because of this, God gave them over to shameful lusts." When we let our desires dictate, as Machiavelli advocated, we pay and pay. This is because uncontrolled desire becomes lust, and lust is insatiable. One can't "feed it so it will go away." To feed lust is to become its slave. It takes over.

The Fall of Society

Uncontrolled desire eventually means an uncontrollable society. So, the fourth and final fall described in Romans 1 is the *fall of society* itself. The passage continues, "He gave them over to a depraved mind, to do what ought not to be done. They have become filled with every kind of wickedness, evil, greed and depravity. They are full of . . . murder, strife, deceit. . . . They invent ways of doing evil; they disobey their parents." These are the things that tear a society apart. The passage continues, "Although they know God's righteous decree that those who do such things deserve death, they not only continue to do these very things but also approve of those who practice them."[21]

Thus, the chapter ends with God describing the judgment people were bringing onto themselves. That the downward spiral should end this way, in judgment, should also be self-evident. No society can survive the loss of its morality. Greed and hatred will tear it apart, even if God doesn't lift a finger against it.

CONCLUSION

Our brief review of history is sobering. It faces us with the fact that we are already living in a society that has cut itself adrift from its moorings, and is searching for a new place to land. As it goes along, it picks up new beliefs and values in an ad hoc fashion with an alarming disregard for truth, or even reason. Romans 1 tells us where we're headed. No society claiming the values this one now espouses has endured. It appears that when a nation crosses a certain threshold of injustice, immorality, and idolatry, God brings it into judgment.[22]

What we see today in our neighbors and friends is not just a passing trend, something that will soon be gone. *The changes in worldview that people are taking on today have the momentum of history behind them.* If we ignore this, or take it lightly, we will fail to discharge our God-given responsibility for our generation. We will fail if we underestimate the distance that actually exists between the unbeliever and faith in Christ. Our response as Christians must be equal to the momentum of the trends we have been talking about.

What is an appropriate response?

CHAPTER THREE

God's People in Society: Why Are We Here?

▼

When the foundations are being destroyed,
what can the righteous do? (Psalm 11:3)

O ur society is moving away from its biblical moorings. The obvious question is, What is the role of those of us who identify ourselves as God's people? What would constitute an appropriate response on our part?

These are critical questions. God's people lay claim to membership in His household and heirdom to His Kingdom. We are participants in His purposes, which span from eternity to eternity. His purposes are at work today, and we are a part of them. Nothing could be more important than to seek a clear understanding of His purposes, of our part, and then to give ourselves to them.

The objective of this chapter is to explore just one facet of God's purposes for His people. What is our present role *in the world*? What are we to be about, and who is responsible to do it? There is really only one place to go for our answers, and that is Scripture.

The conclusions we draw will form the basic thesis of this book. If you agree with them, we can proceed to explore the implications.

GOD'S PEOPLE AND A LOST WORLD: WHY ARE WE HERE?

Several themes run through the Bible that could guide us to the answers we seek. We will look at three of them—first individually, and then braided together to form our thesis.

47

The Scarlet Thread: Redemption and Reconciliation

The theme of redemption and reconciliation runs like a scarlet thread from Genesis to Revelation. To redeem is to buy back something that was formerly yours. To reconcile is to close the distance between parties that have become estranged from one another. We were lost to God at the Fall. No longer were we His. Our rebellion alienated us from Him.

As soon as we fell, God began working to redeem us and to reconcile us to Himself. He signaled the start of this work by seeking out the fallen couple, confronting them with what they had done, and then declaring to Satan that the woman's offspring would deal him a mortal blow.

His next step was to evacuate Adam and Eve from the garden, before they could eat of the Tree of Life.[1] That was critical. Imagine the consequences if they had eaten! Fallen man, living on and on, compounding his evil. If Adam could not have died, he could not have been redeemed. Death became a necessity. It is our exit into eternal life. The Apostle Paul wrote, "Flesh and blood cannot inherit the kingdom of God."[2]

Later the Levitical laws were given as a visual lesson in redemption. They taught the people the difference between the profane and the holy, and that sin has costly consequences that culminate in death. These laws also taught the people that sin demands atonement. The smell of the smoke from the sacrifices that hung over the Israelite camp was a constant reminder of this truth.

Then, through the prophets, the promise came of a suffering Messiah who would be the once-and-for-all Sin-Bearer. So when Jesus approached the Jordan River, John the Baptist called Him "the Lamb of God, who takes away the sin of the world!"[3] God offered Jesus in atonement for our sin.

Those few years that Jesus spent on this earth are the most significant of all history. He is the centerpiece of both human history and of eternity. The life He lived, the death He died, and His victory over it accomplished both the redemption and reconciliation made necessary by the Fall.

This work by Christ was not an emergency plan that God put together when things started to go wrong. Ephesians 1 tells us that even before the foundations of the world were laid, a cross and a people were in His plans. And those plans also include entrusting to His people the ministry of reconciliation of the world. "God . . . reconciled us to himself . . . and gave us the ministry of reconciliation."[4]

The work that God began in Eden and completed in Christ has now been given to us as a holy trust! We have work to do in this unbelieving world. We are a people sent. God made an awesome investment to redeem and reconcile the lost. It is not surprising that He made the communication of this truth a major responsibility.

The Theme of Jesus' Ministry

What is our role in the world? Take a look at the life of Jesus.

Jesus made it clear that the lost were what His coming was really all about. He said, "The Son of Man came to seek and to save what was lost."[5] He risked His reputation among the religious community for the company He kept. People asked, "Why does he eat with tax collectors and 'sinners'?" And He replied, "I have not come to call the righteous, but sinners."[6] The lost were not only the center of His attention, they were central in the things He taught. Luke 15 has been described as "the chapter of lost things." Here Jesus tells three little stories: one of a lost sheep, another of a lost coin, and a third about a lost son. He describes how the shepherd abandoned everything in his anxious search for the lost sheep, and tells of how the woman ransacked her house until she found her coin, and how the father anxiously stood where he could watch the road for his wayward son until he returned. In each case there was a celebration when the lost was found. Jesus said, "In the same way there is more rejoicing in heaven over one sinner who repents than over ninety-nine righteous persons who do not need to repent."[7]

Someone pointed out to me that the one who suffered the loss in each of these parables is God Himself. He is the shepherd, the woman, and the father. In those parables Jesus is describing how God feels. God has suffered a great loss, and He is sparing no effort to recover it.

Given this context of Jesus' life and teachings, the nature of His final commands to His followers hardly comes as a surprise.

"This gospel of the kingdom will be preached in the whole world as a testimony to all nations."[8]

"Go and make disciples of all nations."[9]

"Go into all the world and preach the good news to all creation."[10]

"Repentance and forgiveness of sins will be preached in [my] name to all nations."[11]   STORY I HAVE NO OTHER PLAN.

And He prayed to His Father, "My prayer is not that you take them out of the world but that you protect them. . . . As you sent me into the world, I have sent them into the world . . . so that the world may believe."[12]

We come away from this glimpse at Jesus' life with one obvious observation: We too must perceive ourselves as being in the world for the sake of the lost. It is not the only reason we are here, but it is certainly a major one. This conclusion is virtually identical to the one we came to as we looked at the theme of redemption and reconciliation.

The Glory of God

Any discussion of God's purposes for His people would be incomplete without a look at the subject of God's glory. What's God's purpose for His people? "That's an easy one," we respond. "It's on the first page of every catechism! It is to glorify God." And we have an abundance of scripture to support that answer.

Bring my sons from afar
    and my daughters from the end of the earth—
everyone who is called by my name,
    whom I created for my glory.[13]

And then, "that we, who were the first to hope in Christ, might be for the praise of his glory."[14]

What do we understand that to mean? God is glorious. He has glory. Glory is intrinsic to His being. We grope for synonyms to clarify, but words like *magnificence* and *splendor* are the best we can find.

The truth of God's glory has many profound implications, but there is one facet of it that is very instructive concerning the subject of this chapter. It not only helps define the role of God's people in the world, it identifies the basic means by which that role is to be fulfilled.

"Glorify" according to John. The Apostle John consistently uses the word *glorify* in a simple, singular manner.

He begins his gospel by declaring, "The Word became flesh and lived for a while among us. We have seen his glory, the glory of the one and only Son, . . . full of grace and truth."[15] So from the beginning John establishes the fact that Jesus came so that we, mortal men and women, could be eyewitnesses of the very glory of God. How was that accomplished? As we move on through the book we find the answer to that question in John's usage of the verb *glorify*.

When Jesus told Lazarus' sisters that their brother's illness was "for God's glory so that God's Son may *be glorified* through it,"[16] He was saying that Lazarus' illness, death, and resurrection would prove to reveal certain things about both the Father and about Jesus Himself. Jesus referred to His imminent execution as being His hour to be glorified.[17] Immediately after Judas had been identified as the betrayer, Jesus said, "Now is the Son of Man glorified and God is glorified in him."[18]

How can being betrayed by a friend and being publicly executed possibly be construed to be a glorious event? They cannot be. They are ugly. But both events served to reveal Jesus as indeed the Promised One, sent from God. Judas' betrayal fulfilled a messianic prophecy, and Jesus' death revealed the very heart of God. "This is how we know what love is: Jesus Christ laid down his life for us."[19]

These surprising uses of the verb *glorify* are helpful to our understanding. *Jesus was glorified, and His Father was glorified, whenever any person or event served to reveal something about Him to those around Him.* To reveal Him is to glorify Him.

Jesus' description of the work of the Holy Spirit is also consistent with this definition. He said, "He will bring glory to me by taking from what is mine and making it known to you."[20] It's the same idea. The Holy Spirit's work is to reveal Christ to us.

Why is God so concerned that people get an accurate look at Him—that is, that He be glorified? Jesus helps us understand that question in His prayer of John 17. Here He is talking to His Father about the ordeal He is going through—and looks beyond it to the fruit that will come. He says, "Father, the time has come. Glorify your Son, that your Son may glorify you."[21] What He means is, Father, show people who I really am by the way You take Me through all this, not for My own sake, but so that I might, in turn, reveal You to the world as You really are. Why? Why all this concern for glory? Because "this is eternal life: that they may know you, the only true God, and Jesus Christ, whom you have sent."[22] *He must be accurately revealed (glorified) in order for people to know Him and be saved!*

Jesus extends the same function to us. In His conversation with the Apostle Peter in John 21, He predicted a violent death for Peter. The writer adds, "Jesus said this to indicate the kind of death by which Peter would *glorify* God."[23] Jesus was saying that the way Peter would die, the manner in which he would deal with his own martyrdom, would be fruitful. It would display something of God to the world.

Suffering and glory: a couplet. Over and over again, as in Peter's case, suffering and glory are found together in Scripture. Peter himself said, "For a little while you may have had to suffer grief in all kinds of trials. These have come so that your faith . . . may be proved genuine and may result in praise, glory and honor."[24] In the same vein, the Apostle Paul talks about the necessity of sharing "in his sufferings in order that we may also share in his glory . . . that will be revealed in us."[25] What is this connection between our suffering and our glorifying God?

I heard Josef Tson, a Rumanian pastor, speak on the important place martyrs have in God's purposes. He began by calling our attention to the group of martyrs described in Revelation 6:9 who were asking, "How long, Sovereign Lord . . . until you judge the inhabitants of the earth and avenge our blood?" They were told to "wait a little longer, until [those] . . . who were to be killed as they had been was completed."[26] What was this, Tson asked, a quota of martyrs that God wanted to see filled before the end? Why would God intend such a thing? What good does martyrdom serve?

In answer to his own question, Tson observed that in some places, where spiritual darkness is great, it may require martyrdom for truth to break through. As those who do the killing observe those who die, and the way they die, the killers can only conclude that surely truth is with those who are dying. Jesus' conversation with Pilate serves as a case in point. Jesus said, "For this reason I was born . . . to testify to the truth."[27] Later, one of His executioners exclaimed, "Surely this was a righteous man!"[28] — as have millions since. It doesn't take the extreme suffering of martyrdom to make the point. Whatever the suffering, it is an opportunity for God to reveal His works by giving us the power to overcome it. "Truth," said Tson, "must be observed."[29]

Revealing God. We glorify God, then, by revealing something about Him. Just as the moon could be said to glorify the sun as it reflects its light, so God's people, the light of the world, are called to reflect God's person. And there is an audience. Actually there are two audiences.

The first audience is invisible! "[God's] intent was that now, through the church, the manifold wisdom of God should be made known to the rulers and authorities in the heavenly realms."[30] That is an amazing statement. We can't even see that audience, as it is part of the unseen reality. In Hebrews 12 we see that this audience consists of friends, and in Ephesians 6 find that it included foes as well. Somehow, God's working in His people here and now is having repercussions on the cosmic level! Our salvation reverberates throughout the unseen worlds.

Our other audience is more tangible. Jesus said, "Let your light so shine before men, that they may see your good works and give *glory* to your Father who is in heaven."[31] And Peter instructs us to "live such good lives among the pagans that, though they accuse you of doing wrong, they may see your good deeds and *glorify* God on the day He visits us."[32] Our second audience is the unbelieving world.

So, we conclude, one way in which we "glorify God" in this age is by making Him known. This third theme, God's glory, brings us out in the same place as did the other two. But this theme teaches us much about the nature and breadth of the ministry of reconciliation. Because we can glorify God in all that we do, all of life can be ministry.

All of which converges on a single conclusion: The theme of redemption and reconciliation, that scarlet thread that runs from Genesis to Revelation, leads us to the conclusion that God has given us the ministry of reconciliation. This is the work we have been given to do in this unbelieving world. The theme of Jesus' ministry revealed the same thing—that a primary reason for His coming and for our remaining in this world is to bear witness to the world. Finally, we have taken a look at the practical meaning of the word *glorify*. We observed from this theme as well that we are here to reveal Christ to the world (as well as to the spiritual realm). So we conclude that *God's people are in the world for the sake of the lost*. Again, that is not the sole reason for our being here, but it is certainly a primary one. We have also gained some understanding of how we are to accomplish this purpose. We do it by revealing God's person, His nature, and His work to others.

THE NATURE OF THE MINISTRY

If we are in the world to bear witness to the world, we need to understand the manner by which God intends to accomplish His work through us. We need to discover who is to do this work and how it is to be done.

The Scattering of God's People

We have already observed that glorifying God implies an audience, and that one of our audiences is the unbelieving world. To His Father, Jesus said, "My prayer is not that you take them out of the world but that you protect them from the evil one. . . . As you sent me into the world, I have sent them into the world."[33] God's people belong in the world.

Jesus repeatedly addressed the importance of the sending, or scattering, of His people into the world. One example of this is in Matthew 13 where He gives us the parable of the good seed and the weeds. He said, "The kingdom of heaven is like a man who sowed good seed in his field. But . . . his enemy came and sowed weeds among the wheat. . . . The owner's servants came to him and . . . asked . . . 'Do you want us to go and pull [the weeds] up?' 'No,' he answered . . . 'Let both grow together.'"[34] In explaining this parable He told them that He Himself is the sower, that "the field is the world, and the good seed stands for the sons of the kingdom. The weeds are the sons of the evil one, and the enemy who sows them is the devil."[35] The good seed belongs in the ground, right there alongside the sons of the Evil One. Isn't that a dangerous place to be, we ask? Jesus replies, yes, it is, but I have prayed for them, that they will be protected from the Evil One.

In Mark 4 Jesus elaborates further on the same metaphor. Here He says, "This is what the kingdom of God is like. A man scatters seed on the ground. Night and day, whether he sleeps or gets up, the seed sprouts and grows, though he does not know how. All by itself the soil produces grain—first the stalk, then the head, then the full kernel in the head."[36]

I'm not much of a gardener, but I enjoy trying. Those seed packets with their brilliant pictures of flowers or vegetables are irresistible. Someday, they promise, I too will have a garden that looks like that. So I prepare the ground and empty the seeds into it. At that moment I feel a sense of loss. The seeds have vanished and the empty packet is suddenly worthless—and who knows if anything will grow? Planting is a risk. But there can be no flowers until those seeds go into the ground.

Jesus takes this same metaphor of the seed one step further in John 12. Here He says, "The hour has come for the Son of Man to be glorified. I tell you the truth, unless a kernel of wheat falls to the ground and dies, it remains only a single seed. But if it dies, it produces many seeds." Jesus refers to His own death here—and then extends the context to include anyone who would follow Him. He goes on to explain, "The man who loves his life will lose it, while the man who hates his life . . . will keep it. . . . Whoever serves me must follow me; and where I am, my servant also will be."[37]

What a thought-provoking statement! It is not enough to just spend one's life out there among the weeds. The whole purpose is to bear fruit. But that requires the death of the original seed. For one seed to become many, it must germinate. Its own life must be used up to bring the new growth into existence. Jesus used His own death to prove the point. If He had not died, He would have remained a single seed. And so it is with us. We cannot try to operate on a double agenda, serving Christ with a piece of our lives, and ourselves with the rest. Since we don't even know how fruit comes about, the only thing we can bring to the process is our person. So He says, "Where I am, my servant also will be."[38]

Jesus' words here are very much out of step with this feel-good society of ours. The prevailing message of our day is more to the effect that the chief end of life is to achieve one's full potential, and that every person has a divine right to self-fulfillment. Given the contemporary mood, we'd rather pass over these words of Jesus. But we cannot. They address the very essence of ministry. They define ministry.

What Is Ministry?

Ministry has become such a common term that even the news media has picked it up, using it as they report on the fortunes and misfortunes of our religious leaders. We need a more precise definition for our discussions in this book. We will look here at the following characteristics of ministry as it is described in the Scriptures.

◆ Ministry is serving.
◆ Ministry is incarnational.
◆ Ministry is every believer using what he or she has to serve fellow Christians and the unbeliever.

1. Ministry is serving. In Scripture, *ministry* and *service* are synonymous. There are at least six different Greek words that are translated "servant, serve," and they occur more than 250 times in the New Testament alone. Jesus set the tone for God's people when He said, "The Son of Man did not come to be served, but to serve, and to give his life as a ransom for many."[39] He taught His disciples to think in the same way: "If anyone wants to be first, he must be the very last, and the servant of all."[40]

When we understand ministry as service, suddenly there is

ample opportunity for all. There is always room for one more servant, and service requires little talent. Jesus said that giving a cup of cold water in His name is valued as service. There are many ways to serve. The Apostle Peter gave the instruction, "Each one should use whatever gift he has received to serve others, faithfully administering God's grace in its various forms."[41] Leaders are instructed to serve by preparing "God's people for works of service, so that the body of Christ may be built up."[42]

Now this idea of each one serving with whatever one has sounds random, but there is power in it. Kenneth Latourette attempts to account for the sweep of the gospel across the Graeco-Roman world in the first five centuries. This took place in spite of the ridicule and persecution of God's people. The society was disintegrating, and he observes that the solidarity of the Christians in times of distress stood out. "They cared for their poor and for those of their number imprisoned for their faith. . . . Churches would help one another by gifts of money or food. A Christian . . . would be among friends in whatever city or town he found others of his communion."[43]

In discussing the same phenomenon, F. F. Bruce tells how God's people cared not only for the orphan children of their own members, but also rescued and cared for unwanted infants who were put out to die by their parents. This practice, called "exposure," was very common. In one recorded incident a husband, writing to his expectant wife, said, "If it is a boy, keep it; if a girl, expose it." Christians had the reputation for such things as caring for their sick and taking the bitterness out of slavery. Master and slaves understood that they were equals before God. Bruce concludes, "When we try to account for the increase in the numbers of Christians in those days, in spite of official hostility, we must give due consideration to the impression that behavior of this kind would make on the pagan population."[44] James wrote, "Religion that God our Father accepts as pure and faultless is this: to look after orphans and widows in their distress and to keep oneself from being polluted by the world."[45] To minister is to be a servant who pleases God with service to others. That is possible for anyone.

2. Ministry is incarnational. The definition of *incarnation* is to "embody in the flesh," and this requires living among those to whom we are sent. This was true of Jesus—"The Word became flesh and lived for a while among us. We have seen his glory."[46] It was true for the Apostle Paul: "Our gospel came to you not simply with words, but also with power, with the Holy Spirit and with deep conviction. You know how we lived among you."[47] And it is to be true of us.

Ministry is incarnational by nature. Too often we substitute information for incarnation. We tend to feel we accomplish the ministry by circulating biblical truth. The fact that we live in an information society facilitates this misconception. Circulating information costs time and money, but it doesn't cost us our lives.

As I was writing this chapter, I took a break to travel to a city to look in on some couples who had given themselves to Christ about a month before. They had come to Christ through a mutual friend, who himself was a relatively new believer.

Over the last couple of years this mutual friend had attempted repeatedly to tell his friends of Christ, but their response had always been more negative than positive. Then our friend's health failed. He spent eight months in pain, and died. Speaking for the group, one of these new believers told me, "He never would have gotten us if he hadn't gotten sick. We watched him and saw he was unafraid to die. He was in pain for eight months, but he overrode it through his faith and love for God. Not that he became angelic or anything. He was still the same crusty old friend we had always known. But the man knew where he was going. Those eight months were for us." As long as the witness in this case consisted mainly of words, there was little or no progress toward Christ. But the incarnation of those words made them undeniably true. In the physical death of this friend, he bore spiritual fruit.

Paul said, "I die every day."[48] Physical death happens only once, but death to self is to be a daily affair. We need to choose, every day, whether we will live by faith, available as servants to God, or in self-oriented pursuits. To choose the former will result in Christ's revealing Himself in ways and at times we least expect. To choose the latter is to lead barren, powerless lives.

3. Ministry is every believer using what he or she has to serve one another and the lost. Another truth that becomes apparent in this context is that the ministry really belongs to every believer. We are all to be sown in the world; we all have the life of the Holy Spirit in us, who makes us good seed. Many passages that deal with God's people in the New Testament underscore this truth.

God's people in Romans 12 are described as being a body with each different part serving all the other parts. First Corinthians 12 elaborates further on the same metaphor, showing how our individual differences are essential to the well-being of the whole. Ephesians 4 underscores this by saying that the whole body "grows and builds itself up in love, as each part does its work."[49] The Apostle Peter states the same truth succinctly: "Each one should use whatever gift he has received to serve others, faithfully administering God's grace in its various forms."[50] For many the church has come to be a place to sit and watch. Rather it is to be a people, bound together by the Holy Spirit, each using the Spirit's gifts to help one another look and live like Christ. This demonstration is to be made in the presence of a lost world. No body of believers can fulfill God's purpose for them if they live in isolation from the world. In reality we are already strategically positioned in the world by God Himself: "Each one should retain the place in life that the Lord assigned to him and to which God has called him."[51]

Big Things By Little People

Church history can make discouraging reading. As we will see in succeeding chapters, much of it has been such a mess. The problem with the writing of the history of the church is that the historian records three things: the rise and fall of its institutions, biographical material concerning individuals who for one reason or another caught the attention of the public, and the writings of some of these people. Human nature must be fascinated with size and power. But this fascination has cost us our access to a very significant part of the true history of the church. That part passed ignored and unrecorded even as it happened, because no one deemed it to be newsworthy.

The history of the church, from God's perspective, is a history of the Holy Spirit using little people. It consists of a mustard seed here and there, some yeast hidden in dough, or a seed in the ground. Not many wise or influential people are included. Rather, it has been built on the lowly—the little people. Most of these have lived and died unnoticed, probably feeling in their own hearts that they had never really accomplished much for God with their lives. This history we have lost, but not forever. We will no doubt hear it told us as we stand together before God's throne.

Around the turn of the century a Danish immigrant, Carson Christiansen, settled a farm near Thief River Falls, Minnesota. He was a Christian and once made an effort to influence a neighboring farmer couple, Peter and Anna, who were also Danish immigrants. Peter would have nothing to do with the subject, but Anna responded. She believed in Christ in 1922. Peter and Anna had four sons. In her concern for them, Anna sought out the local grocer, Art Hanson, whom she had heard was also a Christian. She persuaded him to employ one of her four sons, Arnold, a nineteen-year-old. This resulted in Arnold's believing in Christ. Arnold's fiancée, Eva, soon followed.

History does not remember either Carson Christiansen or Art Hanson. Both probably went to their graves thinking their lives had not amounted to much more than a lot of farming and grocery selling. They probably didn't even know they had been good seed. Arnold and Eva married and had six children. I'm one of those six. All six of us are indebted to those two unknown men, as the heritage we received has preserved our marriages and brought all our children, in turn, into God's family. As if that is not cause enough for celebration, the combined witness of our family has resulted in fruit that numbers into the thousands and can be found all over the world. And we too are little people. "The least of you will become a thousand, the smallest a mighty nation. I am the Lord; in its time I will do this swiftly."[52] That is among the most motivating verses in all the Bible for me.

This same story has been replayed countless times over the past two thousand years. But it seldom makes the news, as it is virtually invisible. Because our attention is fixed on Christian institutions and their programs, we do not attach much importance to the little things, like one person reaching out to another. This continues to occur daily all over the world, and we continue to deem it incidental. What do you suppose would happen if we turned our priorities around and made enabling one another to serve God by serving people our primary focus?

CONCLUSIONS

In this chapter we have seen that God is in pursuit of this society and that we, His people, are key players in that pursuit. We can summarize our observations with two statements. And with these statements we have our answers to the questions we asked as we embarked on this chapter: What is our present role in the world? And, who is responsible to do it?

1. God's people are in the world to bear witness to the world. We are to live among our unbelieving neighbors, serving them, revealing Christ to them.
2. This ministry depends upon every believer. We are all to use whatever we have to serve God by serving our brothers and sisters and the unbeliever.

These two statements are central biblical truths concerning God's people in society.

Nothing really new there, you might be thinking. You've heard these things taught countless times in the past. Most of us have. But truth is not given to increase our knowledge. It is to be lived. These truths call for a response on our part. And that is what is difficult.

In the history of the church, the times when these two truths were in full practice were rare. The contemporary church seldom focuses on equipping every believer for the ministry of revealing Christ to the people around him or her. That is a primary reason why the mainstream of our society, which is spiritually adrift, is beyond our reach.

In the next three chapters we will explore the past and present to see how the church has handled these two truths. This

excursion will give us insights as we see how they were successfully worked out in the past, and will also help us understand
how it happened that the church has moved away from them.
These chapters will help us see the present in a new light. They
will enable us to see why we are the way we are today, and will
help indicate the direction we must take if we are to bring these
truths back to life.

Part II
FROM ACTS TO THE PRESENT: AN HISTORICAL REVIEW

In chapter 2 we looked into history to understand the origins of our secular society. In this section we will take a more extensive tour of our history, but this time we watch for something different.

We ended the previous chapter by drawing two conclusions about the role of God's people in the world. We concluded that

- ◆ God's people are in the world to bear witness to the world. They are to live among their unbelieving neighbors, serving them, revealing Christ to them.
- ◆ Ministry depends upon every believer. We are all to use whatever we have to serve God by serving one another and the unbeliever.

Then we observed that, in the history of the church, the times when these two truths were in full practice were rare, a fact that holds true of our churches today.

Recently, I spent several days with seven laymen from four different cities in what used to be the Soviet Union. We met because of our mutual commitment to making Christ known to those around us. For the past decade these men had been actively involved with unbelievers, sharing their faith. Their efforts had been fruitful, but they were dealing with a common problem. All seven had been expelled from their churches for having "unauthorized associations with unbelievers"!

Extreme, you say? Not really. It wasn't too long ago that one of my teenage daughters came to me in tears because she had been reprimanded by a youth pastor because of her friendships with nonChristians. She asked, "Dad, is it wrong for me to love my nonChristian friends?"

We went to the second greatest commandment to straighten things out: "'Love your neighbor as yourself.' All the Law and the Prophets," said Jesus, "hang on these . . . commandments."[1]

Even then, Jesus' questioner wasn't comfortable with the idea of being a friend of sinners. Looking for a loophole, he asked, "Who is my neighbor?"[2] In response, Jesus told a story about an unfortunate person who was beaten, robbed, and left half dead. It is people like that, Jesus was saying, that are your neighbors. This helped my daughter keep on track.

But these examples of being out of touch with these truths are mild compared with what we will see in our excursion through history. This excursion, spanning almost two thousand years, will be divided into three parts: New Testament times, from the Church Fathers to the Reformation, and our contemporary church. The diagram on page 65 charts our course.

You cringe, perhaps? Ignatius? Irenaeus? Cyprian? Could the American church's dilemma stem from decisions made less than two hundred years after the Resurrection? Could Augustine have made unbiblical mistakes, and if he could have, could they possibly matter in the twenty-first century AD?

The answer is, yes. If you are a pragmatist and merely want to cut to the bottom line—what should we do differently?—then you should skip chapter 5. But if you want to understand *why* we are in our current situation and why two thousand years of momentum is pushing against needed critical changes, then you should read chapters 4–6 carefully.

You may already have the vision for quartz watches, but part 2 of the book will explain why so many wise and godly people find it hard to stop thinking gears and springs.

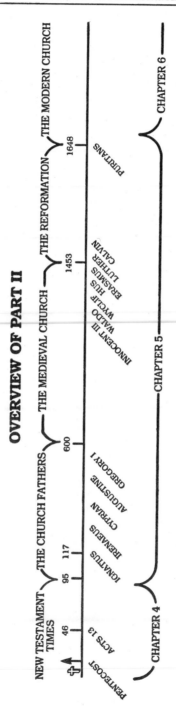

OVERVIEW OF PART II

CHAPTER FOUR

How Did the Gospel Grow? An Historical Look at the New Testament

▼

I t can be done! God's people can go to the world and every believer can be fruitfully involved in the enterprise. The value of a chapter spanning the period of New Testament history (about thirty-two years) is that it shows us not only that they did it, but how they did it. This chapter will hold some surprises as we examine the dynamics of the growth of the gospel in this period.

FROM JERUSALEM TO ANTIOCH

This period, which is described in Acts 1–12, spans about fourteen years. It is a unique time, a once-in-history situation. Leadership was provided primarily by the original apostles, and the focus was almost entirely on the Jews.

God had indeed prepared the Jewish community for its Messiah. Over a period of twenty centuries He had covenanted with the Jewish people. He had given them the Law, the Temple, and a succession of prophets. Jesus told the apostles that He would send them to reap what they had not worked for. They would go where others had done the hard work of planting and cultivating. They would reap the benefits of other people's labor. And so it happened. The audience that Peter addressed in Acts 2 is described as being "God-fearing Jews from every nation under heaven."[1] These were people who had the Word of God: the writings of Moses and the prophets, and the Psalms. They knew the stories and embraced the promises of a Messiah that would come. It was an in-house affair, Jews to fellow Jews. In his message, Peter could skip the details of the historical events and get to the point: Jesus. And no one asked, "Jesus who?" They all knew about Him. Many had listened to Him themselves. Some undoubtedly had even been healed by Him as He went from village to village. He "was a man accredited by God to you by miracles, wonders and signs, which God did among you through him."[2] Some had even been party to His death.

Now here was this little group of 120 followers of Jesus, claiming to be eyewitnesses to His resurrection. They were all Galileans but were speaking the languages and dialects of the surrounding regions and nations. It is not surprising that three thousand believed on that day!

That was just the beginning. Every day from then on, more people believed. The growth was so rapid that soon Jerusalem was filled with the teachings about Jesus. The energizing force behind this explosion in Jerusalem was the Holy Spirit, who emboldened every person to speak about Christ. He gave them a spirit of unity and generosity, and He enhanced their credentials by empowering them to perform miracles.

Their message also made them unstoppable. To paraphrase, it was, "You killed Him, God raised Him, and we've seen Him and talked with Him." The Resurrection was their focal point. Some were eyewitnesses to the fact that the grave was empty on that Sunday morning, and many others from both Judea and Galilee had seen Jesus alive. It wasn't just the empty tomb that they preached. Their message was also that they had found the living Christ.

Another quality that made these first followers of Christ irresistible was their level of mutual commitment, their solidarity. They were devoted to one another to the point of holding their earthly possessions in common. They shared everyday life together. The power of their fellowship apparently both intimidated and attracted the unbelieving world. Luke writes, "No one else dared join them, even though they were highly regarded by the people.

Nevertheless, more and more men and women believed in the Lord and were added to their number."[3]

I wonder how those first believers understood what was going on. For many, it must have been seen as Judaism finally come true. It probably never entered their minds that Judaism was to decline almost to a vanishing point within a few decades, and that they were, in fact, a part of a new global work by God. Their activities centered around the Temple as they held to the traditional daily prayer schedule of the Temple and continued to observe the Jewish customs and feasts. They had no thought of separating themselves from the rest of Israel. For them it was simple. The ancient Scriptures had been fulfilled.

Others obviously had more insight into what was really afoot. A young Hellenist, Stephen, must have recognized that it would be impossible for this message to remain within the boundaries of Judaism. He must have recognized that the Temple, with its rituals and institutions, was now obsolete. He was arrested and brought before the Sanhedrin under the charge that he spoke "against this holy place and against the law," that he had said, "Jesus of Nazareth will destroy this place and change the customs of Moses handed down to us."[4] Stephen got along okay in his defense before the Sanhedrin until he got to the part about the Temple. His quotation from Amos cost him his life:

> Heaven is my throne,
>   and the earth is my footstool.
> What kind of house will you build for me?
>   says the Lord.
> Or where will my resting place be?
> Has not my hand made all these things?[5]

Stephen was saying the same thing Jesus had told the Samaritan woman, that the time "has now come when the true worshipers will worship the Father in spirit and truth";[6] that Jerusalem was no longer the place. This rejection of the Temple, the priesthood, and everything associated with those institutions formed the basis for a charge of blasphemy by the Sanhedrin. Stephen was stoned to death.

Apparently many believers in Jerusalem couldn't grasp the significance of what Stephen said. Not only did they continue to embrace both the gospel and their Jewish customs, they insisted that these things were essential to the gospel for all believers.

With the first outbreak of persecution, recorded in Acts 8, God's people had to flee Jerusalem. Leaving Jerusalem meant leaving the Temple. Thus the Temple ceased to be the focal point of the fledgling movement. This liberated the gospel from the Temple and extended it geographically.

Those believers who fled Jerusalem demonstrated great energy and courage. All were scattered by persecution of the gospel, but they preached the gospel wherever they went. As they seized every occasion, the message spread throughout Judea and Samaria. No one was concerned with authorization from the top. Whatever seemed to be a good idea at the time is what they did. Philip went to Samaria and saw great response. Peter and John heard about it in Jerusalem and went to help him. Next Philip helped an Ethiopian understand and believe in Christ. After that, he just went about from town to town preaching Christ. Apparently a lot of this sort of thing went on, as by the time Saul was converted, God's people had spread into Judea, Galilee, Samaria, Phoenicia, Cyprus, and Antioch.

There was great freedom, and the Holy Spirit used those early Christians, intoxicated as they were with the fact of the risen Christ, to fill the surrounding regions with the news. But there were limits, limits that were self-imposed. Those who had been scattered by the persecution had confined their message only to Jews! "Now those who had been scattered . . . traveled as far as Phoenicia, Cyprus and Antioch, telling the message only to Jews."[7] There had been some exceptions to this, but by and large God's people had not ventured out beyond their own culture. Dynamic though they were, God's people were culture-bound. We will be examining this phenomenon in more depth as we go along. For now, we want to make a single observation: Had the movement of the gospel been left to proceed following the same pattern, it would have been disastrous to the future of its growth. The movement would soon have run out of steam.

The gospel of Christ quickly permeated the Jewish world.

There was a great ingathering. But all of this would have stopped as soon as it reached the outer limits of the Jewish world. The gospel would have become culture-bound, confined as a Jewish sect. *Only as it was extricated from Jewish beliefs and customs was the message free to become the good news for all nations as it was intended to be.* So what happened next in the growth of the gospel was absolutely critical.

Summary

We have seen that as the gospel made its first surge, filling Jerusalem and then spilling over into Judea and Samaria, it was carried *by* Jews almost exclusively *to* Jews. This was done purposefully, as most of those early believers understood what was transpiring as the actual fulfillment of the messianic prophecies. Jesus was the promised Messiah, and the Jewish believers tended to interpret that fact in nationalistic terms. For example, the final question the apostles asked Jesus was political: "Lord, are you at this time going to restore the kingdom to Israel?"[8] They were not prepared to think beyond their own nation, or their own kind.

THE APOSTOLIC EFFORT: ACTS 13–28

A very significant aspect of this first surge of the gospel, from Jews to Jews, is to be found in the exceptions to that norm. These exceptions began to reveal God's intention for the rest of the world.

The Apostle Peter's visit to the Italian military officer in Caesarea is one of these exceptions. Peter went under coercion by the Holy Spirit, and when he returned to Jerusalem he found himself in trouble with his fellow Jews for what he had done. Another exception was the spread of the gospel to Antioch. About ten years after things began in Jerusalem, some people of Cyprus and Cyrene went to Antioch and began to offer the gospel to the Greeks of that city.

The response in Antioch was significant enough to attract the attention of the leaders in Jerusalem. They sent Barnabas to see what was going on. He was delighted with what he found and immediately went after reinforcements, and he knew where to look. He went to Tarsus to recruit the maverick Pharisee, Saul. Saul had been converted a few years earlier and had nearly gotten himself killed twice for preaching Christ to Jews. He had to be sent away from Jerusalem because of the turmoil he generated. It was probably an open secret that Saul was busy preaching the gospel to Gentiles up there in Tarsus.

So Acts 13 opens with the leaders in Antioch meeting together. They were an unusual mix of "prophets and teachers."[9] Barnabas was a Levite from Cyprus; Simeon was called Niger, or "black"; Lucius was Cyrenian; Manaen was a Greek raised in Herod's court, a schoolmate of Herod Antipas; and there was the Jew, Saul of Tarsus. As these men were together worshiping the Lord, the Holy Spirit enlisted two of them, Barnabas and Saul, for a new enterprise. He was forming an apostolic team. From then on Barnabas and Saul were referred to as apostles rather than prophets or teachers. They had changed their function in the body.

Soon after Barnabas and Saul set out on their first journey, Saul dropped his Jewish name and started using his Latin one, Paul (as a Roman citizen he had to have a legal Latin name). The Roman name sounded better to Gentile ears. The two went from city to city, stopping first in the synagogues to reap the fruit of the labors of the patriarchs and prophets. They would go wherever they could get a hearing and stay as long as it was physically safe to do so—which often wasn't very long. Or, as in Ephesus, the stay would stretch into years, until the task of teaching "the whole will of God"[10] was completed and the foundations of leadership were laid.

There were a number of apostolic teams in those days. The one we know the most about is Paul's. Paul and Barnabas split up over a disagreement. Barnabas teamed up with Mark, and Paul chose Silas as his new companion. Timothy soon joined Paul and Silas as well. At one point Paul's team numbered at least eight men. Paul would depend upon these men to go wherever they were needed, to complete whatever had been left unfinished. Sometimes Paul would send a trusted man like Timothy in his place when he was unable to go himself.[11]

One of the most outstanding things about Paul was the clarity of his vision. He knew his purpose. He knew where he needed to go, where to start when he got there, who to talk to, what to say and do, and he knew when he was done!

Paul knew he was sent to the Gentiles. He knew he was to go from city to city, and he made it a point to go to the unreached. In Romans 15 he said, "So from Jerusalem all the way around to Illyricum, I have fully proclaimed the gospel of Christ. It has always been my ambition to preach the gospel where Christ was not known. . . . But now," he continues, "there is no more place for me to work in these regions."[12]

I find this incredible. Paul was saying he had finished his work in all the regions to the east of Italy. He was making plans now to carry the gospel to Spain, and hoped to stop in Rome on his way and engage the Roman believers in that new enterprise. What did he mean, he had finished? Is he implying that he had preached the gospel to every breathing soul from Jerusalem to Illyricum? Certainly not.

When Paul went to a new city he had limited objectives. He didn't try to do everything. Rather, he viewed himself as a foundation layer. His part of the work was done as soon as there were people who were rooted and growing in Christ and *who were, in turn, carrying the gospel forward.* He evaluated his efforts as successful only when it was evident that the gospel had taken root and was continuing to grow, even in his absence.

This is what Paul was getting at when he wrote to the Corinthians, "We . . . will confine our boasting to the field God has assigned to us, a field that reaches even to you. . . . Our hope is that, as your faith continues to grow, our area of activity among you will greatly expand, so that we can preach the gospel in the regions beyond you."[13] Paul recognized that the real impact of the gospel in a region would not be made by an apostolic team that would come in and then leave. It would be made by those left behind: the insiders, the people of a society who had become believers. Apparently Paul watched these fledgling believers to see if this new life was really going to continue to grow. When it did he would breathe a sigh of relief—and turn his attention to the next frontier. There was a dynamic interdependence between

Paul's mobile apostolic efforts and the local efforts of the seedling fellowships he established. He communicated this same interdependence as he wrote to the Christians in Philippi, "Do everything without complaining or arguing, so that you may become blameless and pure . . . in a crooked and depraved generation, in which you shine like stars in the universe as you hold out the word of life—in order that I may boast on the day of Christ that I did not run or labor for nothing."[14]

Here's an example we can profit from. Those believers understood that they were in the world as witnesses to the unbelieving world. They also understood that the basic means of getting to that world was in their living out the gospel as a community in a lost society. Paul helped them keep their mission in focus, and also helped them understand that their faithfulness on the local level had a direct bearing on how far the gospel would expand through the apostolic effort. Once there was evidence that the gospel had truly taken root and would continue to bear fruit, the apostolic team felt released to move on to the regions beyond.

Crossing Cultural Boundaries

It is hard for us to appreciate the extent of the cultural chasm that separated first-century Jews from their Gentile surroundings. We will be looking at this more closely in chapter 7. For now it is sufficient to give one example. In the Acts 10 account of Peter's visit to Cornelius, we find Peter saying to his Gentile host, "You are well aware that it is against our law for a Jew to associate with a Gentile or visit him."[15] Can you imagine saying something like this to your host?

Where did Peter get that idea? He did not get it out of the Old Testament, nor did Jesus ever tell him anything like that. It is a part of "The Tradition of the Elders," that body of teaching that came from the Jewish scribes of the day. Simon Peter, perhaps the key mover among the believers in those early days, struggled against his own ethnocentrism as he watched the gospel grow. (Ethnocentrism is the belief in the inherent superiority of one's own group and culture.) Given our natural tendencies, it is not hard to understand the importance of a cross-cultural apostolic team like the Apostle Paul's.

The gospel never would have broken out and made its way around the world without the apostolic team. The apostolic effort was, in the main, God's people moving into the unbelieving world. The Holy Spirit has chosen to tell us very little about what happened after Pentecost to most of the Twelve, but He has left us a detailed record of Paul's efforts. Certainly this was purposeful. Paul was the consummate cross-cultural messenger, cross-cultural in the way he thought and in the message he preached.

Paul Johnson emphasizes Paul's qualification as a cross-cultural apostle, both in personal background and in the diversity of cultural experience in the city of Tarsus.[16] Paul was born a pure Jew, of the tribe of Benjamin, circumcised on the eighth day. He was a fourth-generation Pharisee, a fervent keeper of Jewish law, trained in the rabbinical school in Jerusalem.

Johnson tells us Paul's "family had moved to Tarsus at the time of the Roman occupation, had become wealthy Roman citizens, but remained pillars of the conformist diaspora [the communities of practicing Jews outside Palestine]."[17] Tarsus was a cosmopolitan city, called the "Athens of Asia Minor." It was a crossroads in more ways than one—in commerce, culture, and religion. Of course Paul spoke both Greek and Aramaic. Paul was a product of diversity, but it took his conversion to explode his conservative commitment to the rabbinic interpretations of the Law and transform him into a man who could be all things to all men. The key to Paul's crossing cultural boundaries was his willingness to leave behind the traditions in which he had been raised.

The Cross-Cultural Message
Paul was the first to clearly understand Jewish law and tradition as distinct from the gospel of Christ. This understanding was not of his own invention. It was revealed to him. Paul refers to "the mystery made known to me by revelation."[18] His message, he insisted, "is not something that man made up. I did not receive it from any man, nor was I taught it; rather, I received it by revelation from Jesus Christ."[19] He also pointed out that this mystery message "was not made known to men in other generations."[20]

What was the big secret? Paul explains: "Through the gospel the Gentiles are heirs together with Israel . . . sharers together in the promise in Christ Jesus."[21] Not much of a surprise, you say. But at that point in the history of God's people it was a wild, revolutionary idea. This revelation made the gospel a message for all nations because it could be carried about the world unencumbered by Jewish religious and cultural traditions. This clear-eyed understanding of the gospel is what made Paul so unique.

The Cross-Cultural Messenger

Cross-cultural apostles possess the ability to understand the receiver and communicate the pure truth of the gospel in terminology that is familiar to that person. They are able to show how this gospel addresses needs and how it will deliver a person from the things he or she fears and struggles with the most. They are also able to help those who respond to reorder their lives around Christ and His truth.

This ability to carry the gospel from one culture to another without distorting its meaning in the process is rare. All of us are by nature ethnocentric. We all tend to measure others against ourselves, as if our ways and our experiences are the criteria of what is right and wrong, good and bad. Occasionally someone comes along who has the ability to keep his or her own ways in a more balanced perspective and thereby truly accept people who are dissimilar. This absence of judgment is immediately sensed by those on the receiving end.

The Apostle Paul was the consummate cross-cultural messenger. He could be a Jew among the Jews. He could observe the traditions when among people who felt they were important. With a different crowd, he could set those same traditions aside and not feel ill at ease. He was weak among the weak. He did whatever was most conducive to putting at ease those he was seeking to win.[22] It takes this ability if the purity of the gospel is to be preserved as it is carried across cultural boundaries.

Talk about a contemporary need! Where are the apostles today? Gone, we say. For many, apostleship died with the original twelve. As John Hannah put it, "We were so awed by the original twelve, we retired the number." What about that? Can we write off this essential function as a thing of the past?

THE APOSTOLIC FUNCTION

The term *apostle* is used in several distinct ways in the New Testament. The Twelve were obviously a unique and unrepeatable bridge between the life and work of Jesus and the establishing of His people. They were given special authority. The Apostle Paul was also unique for reasons we have just examined. Primarily, his uniqueness lay in his special calling to the Gentiles, and in the revelations given him concerning the message for the Gentile world.

But the subject of apostleship does not end here. A number of other New Testament people were referred to as apostles. These people did not carry the same unique credentials or authority. They held no position or office. It was their work, or function, that was apostolic. There was even room for "false apostles"—an impossibility if the term had been reserved for just twelve men. Barnabas, Apollos, Silas, Timothy, and Epaphroditus are all referred to as apostles in the New Testament.[23] They were thus described because of the kind of work they were doing. So, we ask, how did people in New Testament times understand apostleship?

In New Testament times, *apostle* was a simple everyday word that meant "to send." It was used for things; we "apostle" a Federal Express package. It was also used for people, a delegate or messenger, "one sent forth with orders." In New Testament usage, the word *apostle* is used to describe a person who does a certain kind of work. It does not connote position. It does not necessarily imply being cross-cultural.[24] The description of functions in Ephesians should be understood in this light. Paul wrote, "It was he who gave some to be apostles, some to be prophets, some to be evangelists, and some to be pastors and teachers, to prepare God's people for works of service, so that the body of Christ may be built up."[25]

I don't think Ephesians 4 is intended to describe a single fellowship of believers in a corner of Ephesus, or even the composite of the various fellowships in that city. Paul is describing the functions that need to be present or available to the people of God if they are to discharge their calling. He is saying, "You're going to need help from people who are gifted to serve as apostles, prophets, evangelists, pastors, and teachers if you really expect to see every believer engaged in serving and in building up the body. You will need the apostle with his vision for the whole, and his ability to make new things happen. You will need the prophet with his special ability to interpret the times in the context of God's Word. The evangelist is necessary to help you in your own sowing and reaping. You're going to need the gentle, and sometimes not-so-gentle, care of the shepherd to stay encouraged and on track. And the teacher will help you live according to God's truth."

We cannot live healthy lives as God's people if we neglect any of these functions. We need to accept these people as gifts, all of them, from the Holy Spirit to God's people. When we do that, the passage concludes, "The whole body, joined and held together by every supporting ligament, grows and builds itself up in love, as each part does its work."[26]

THE NATURAL EXPANSION OF GOD'S PEOPLE: THE EPISTLES

We have just seen how the apostolic effort had a critical but limited part in the growth of the gospel in the world. We will now see how the local expressions of the body also have a distinctive but limited part. Every part of the body has limits. No individual or group is to do everything. If we don't know our limits, we won't know where to begin, what to do, or when our work is finished. It is liberating for a body of believers to know their God-given limits.

One wonders what it must have been like to have been a part of that first nucleus of believers in a city like Thessalonica or Corinth. I think perhaps it was something like this:

Suddenly, unannounced and out of nowhere, a half-dozen men arrived in our town. Their first stop was the syna-gogue—a place where the Jews and a few proselytes observe their religion. They created such an uproar with their teaching that they split the congregation and got themselves thrown out of the synagogue. They then resorted to the homes of their converts, where they continued to teach. Neighbors and family members were attracted; so many of us believed that it became the talk of the town. Opposition began to mount as both the civil and religious leaders of the city began to fear for the stability of their respective institutions. There were some arrests, some beatings, until finally the team was forced to move on. But somewhere along the line we heard and understood what these men said about Jesus. We observed the messengers' love for Him and for one another. We discovered to our amazement that the visitors loved us with the same love and treated us with integrity. Their teaching struck an inner chord with us. It addressed a chronic longing. So we took this Jesus to ourselves as our only God. As the pressure mounted against these visitors, and against some of us, we feverishly seized every opportunity to learn everything we could from them. We wore them out in our hunger to know more. Suddenly they were gone and we were alone. Some of our number had learned enough to continue to teach the rest of us. Others had emerged as leaders. Some of our homes had become the focal point of activities. We had become like a giant family, with all of us helping with whatever we were able to do. Strangely, we did not feel abandoned. The Holy Spirit was in us and among us, teaching and changing us in ways we would not have believed possible.

An apostolic team had passed through the city like a combine, reaping all who were prepared to respond: Jews, proselytes, God-fearers, and others in whom the Spirit of God had been working. This nucleus of new life faced two immediate tasks. Perhaps these are timeless: the two immediate priorities for any new body of believers.

Changed Lives

The first task was delivering believers from the corruption of the world out of which they had been saved. Paul put it graphically when he said, "I promised you to one husband, to Christ, so that

I might present you as a pure virgin to him."[27] New believers need help if they are to break free of the inertia of a lifetime of destructive habits. They need to break free and then go on, continuing to change until they truly resemble Christ Himself.

Those early Christians faced a formidable task in this area. Paul described the believing community in Corinth as being ex-idolaters, adulterers, prostitutes, homosexual offenders, thieves, drunkards, and swindlers. They weren't exactly the beautiful people about town. How could such people be transformed into a holy bride, fit for Christ Himself? We will be looking at this more closely in chapter 9.

Witness to the World

The second task of these new believers was to influence their world with this good news. Paul wrote to the Ephesians, "For you were once darkness, but now you are light in the Lord. Live as children of light. . . . Have nothing to do with the fruitless deeds of darkness. . . . It is light that makes everything visible. . . . Be very careful, then, how you live—not as unwise but as wise, making the most of every opportunity, because the days are evil."[28]

This passage expresses the central idea of the epistles concerning the way believers in a local situation were to fulfill their responsibility to the world around them. They were not to be passive, nor were they to withdraw from society. They were to have a sense of mission toward those around them, but the tactics they were instructed to employ were different from those employed by the apostolic team.

On no occasion did any of the writers of the epistles tell believers to go back to the synagogue and shake it up one more time. Nor were they told to preach in the town square. They were not told to go door to door. Not that these things would have been wrong. It's that they would not have proven fruitful. The combine had just passed through the city, reaping those who were prepared. To run the combine over the same field a second time would not be productive.

That nucleus of new believers constituted the seed corn for the future. They had been planted by the apostolic team, and were expected to result in continued fruitfulness. This was achieved as those believers lived such good lives among the pagans that truth was revealed. When people see the truth lived out, they want to hear what we have to say. And what they hear makes sense because of what they have seen. The relevance of the truth becomes undeniable. The new crop is harvested in due season, but the mode of farming, this time, is very different from that practiced by an apostolic team. It involves tilling the soil, planting, cultivating, watering, and finally harvesting.

By and large the apostolic function has passed into disuse among us today. This is a calamitous loss as it leaves the local church attempting to do everything. This loss causes confusion and a sense of failure among our people. For example, when average believers think of getting involved with the lost, they think they have to emulate the Apostle Paul. They interpret "being a witness" as becoming one-person assault squads with the gospel, and that is just too daunting. As a result they give up and focus on safer "in-house" chores that need to be done within the church. No one has ever told them there might be another mode of outreach that would fit them far better, and would allow them to participate fruitfully in God's purposes throughout their lifetime. We will expand on this in the final chapters.

CONCLUSION

As we traced the progress of God's people in the New Testament, we saw how the apostolic and local efforts were inseparable. Each was dependent upon the other. One would have failed without the other. The apostolic effort made new plantings. The local bodies nurtured those plantings and brought them to maturity and fruitfulness. The apostolic teams were "on call," praying, corresponding, and sending people to serve the needs of God's people. The apostolic team's ongoing commitment was to complete whatever was lacking among the local bodies. They helped believers break open the natural opportunities that surrounded them. The local believers strengthened the apostolic effort by supplying people, funds, and hospitality. They colabored in prayer. The two were interdependent, yet neither attempted to own or to control the other. The authority on either side was earned and voluntary, the product of mutual trust and commitment. Sometimes there were tensions and conflicts between the two. But much of the gospel's expansion in New Testament times has to be attributed to the cooperation of these two expressions of God's people.

Kenneth Scott Latourette reaches the same conclusion, drawing upon an early Christian document, the *Didache Ton Dodeka Apostolon*, or *Teaching of the Twelve Apostles*, as a resource. This document "describes a church organization which knew of traveling apostles and prophets and of resident prophets and teachers. It instructs the Christians to appoint for themselves bishops and deacons and to hold them in honor, along with the prophets and teachers. . . . In any event, the latter part of the first century and the fore part of the second century still saw variety in the forms of organization of the churches."[29]

Apostles, prophets, evangelists, pastors, and teachers are listed in Ephesians 4:11 as being essential to the life of God's people. It took the full spectrum of these functions, some "traveling," some "scattering," and others "resident," for God's people to fulfill their mission to this first-century generation. It requires the same today.

One of our contemporary weaknesses is the belief that a single local fellowship can be self-sufficient. We tend to ignore the truth that the believers in a city are spiritually linked together under one Head. Fraternal love should characterize the relationships between fellowships. Also, fellowships that do not have ongoing input from people who minister on a broader-than-local level suffer spiritual myopia. They need more than occasional reports from such people; they need them around long enough to be equipped in the skills they have gained along the way. Without this they will miss the benefit of the contemporary expression of the apostolic function, and will be unskilled for their own efforts in natural expansion.

CHAPTER FIVE

From Ignatius to the Puritans: AD 95–1620

▼

The experience of God's people in the first century proves that every believer can be fruitfully involved in the enterprise of going into all the world. But even in that first time around, the accomplishment of that ideal required a sensitive balancing among those who exercised the various necessary functions. Things got tense at times, and were it not for the humility of the leaders, the differences could have generated serious conflicts. The voluntary mutual submission of authority between apostolic leaders and elders preserved the unity and enabled the ministry.

Now we will see what happened after that first generation moved off the scene. The scope of this chapter spans fifteen centuries. We will begin with Ignatius, one of the Church Fathers and a contemporary of the Apostle John. Then we will look at several other leaders scattered in time across the centuries. Each of the people I have chosen affected God's people in the area of our concern for better or worse. The chapter will end with the first boatloads of Puritans making their way from England to America.

The question we will be seeking to answer as we make our way through the centuries remains the same: How did the church do against our thesis? How did the church do in going to the world? What place did the average believer have in its ministry?

History being what it is, and my limitations being what they are, I embark on this chapter with apprehension. Will and Ariel Durant devoted their lives to the study of history. Their eleven-volume *The Story of Civilization* is a historical monument in itself. But upon reflecting back on their life's work, they said, "'Most history is guessing, and the rest is prejudice.' Even the historian who thinks to rise above partiality for his country, race, creed, or class betrays his secret predilection in his choice of materials, and in the nuances of his adjectives. The historian always oversimplifies, and hastily selects a manageable minority of facts and faces out of a crowd of souls and events whose multitudinous complexity he can never quite embrace or comprehend.'"[1]

I will be doing in this chapter what the Durants warn against, as I am interested in tracing the progression of a single facet of the church through history. Certainly I will be guilty of oversimplifying as I select my "manageable minority of facts and faces" out of the crowds that make up history. I have hesitations in attempting to span so much history with such a brief treatment. I realize the things I leave unsaid can easily strip what I do say of its proper context. But I will proceed, as I see no other way to lay the foundations for the observations I will subsequently be making. We need to understand where it was that God's people first lost their ability to go to the world, and why it happened. Hopefully I will not be misleading.

I will narrow this chapter's focus in yet another way. Tradition indicates that the first disciples, together with other early Christians, moved out in all directions once things were broken up in Jerusalem. As they moved into the nations, they gave birth to a rich variety of Christian traditions. Our focus here will be on just one branch of that expansion—that which gave origin to the Western church, which eventually found its way to North America.

PERSECUTION AND HERESIES FROM WITHOUT; HERESIES AND DIVISIONS FROM WITHIN

In the previous chapter we saw how Judaism served as the cradle for God's people for the first decade or more. This worked to their advantage within the Roman Empire, since the Jews enjoyed a unique exemption from the state religion, which included the obligation of emperor worship. For a time the Roman state treated believers in Christ as just one more sect under the umbrella of Judaism, extending to them the same exemption. Michael Green deals thoroughly with these early developments in his book, *Evangelism in the Early Church*, from which I have drawn heavily in this section.[2]

Those first Jewish believers needed that time of relative peace as everything was new and unclear. Certainly many of them weren't clear themselves on what they were into, or where it was all taking them. They had grown up on the stories of the Patriarchs—Abraham, Isaac, and Jacob—and of David, the shepherd-king. They knew David's throne was to be eternal and that the Messiah would one day sit upon it. Now, that Messiah had come. His manner of coming had taken everyone by surprise. He had not come as a king at all. Most had thought He was a prophet. When He died, everyone assumed it was all over. But His resurrection had proven that He was, indeed, the Messiah! And after His resurrection, He Himself had, on more than one occasion, shown some of them from the Scriptures how it all fit together.

But what were they becoming now? Were they still a part of Judaism, or were they something else? And what about Moses and the Law? Was all that just to be ignored and forgotten? Hard questions these, the kind that generate strong feelings in every direction. Tensions ran high over these issues among those first-century believers. But the inner tensions were nothing compared to the threats from without.

God's people were persecuted and finally disavowed by the Jewish society. Once disavowed they became vulnerable to the Roman powers. Nero's brutal tortures of Christians in AD 64 was the first of a series of waves of persecution. Christians were not respected by society. They were generally regarded as odd, socially unprofitable people who were suspected of everything from incest to cannibalism. They had the reputation of being dangerous, anti-social beings, politically disloyal to the state. To join them meant to court martyrdom.

The philosophical environment in which these believers had to live added to their woes. *Gnosticism* thrived in the then-fashion-able Greek way of thinking, which accepted rational analysis as the way to truth. Gnosticism carried reason to its extreme, concluding that spirit and matter had little connection with one another. The flesh was evil, the pure spirit, good. "Gnostics had two central preoccupations: belief in a dual world of good and evil and belief in the existence of a secret code of truth."[3] It was eclectic, incorporating whatever "truth" had been discovered in any of the faiths.

Believers in Christ had to cope with a number of philosophies of similar gender, such as Neoplatonism and Manichaeanism, and were not immune to their influences. Paul Johnson said, "So far as we can judge, by the end of the first century, and virtually throughout the second, the majority of Christians believed in varieties of Christian-gnosticism, or belonged to revivalist sects grouped round charismatics."[4] And, "Even in Antioch, where both Peter and Paul had been active, there seems to have been confusion until the end of the second century. Antioch harbored a multitude of esoteric religious cults. Gnosticism was powerful, and may have taken over Christianity after the departure of the apostles."[5]

To mix Gnosticism with the gospel was to destroy the gospel. Since spirit was good and flesh was corrupt, according to Gnosticism, Christ could never have become flesh at all. He merely seemed to be a man, while in reality He was pure spirit. So the truth about Christ was lost. Asceticism (control of the body) replaced faith.

Salvation was understood to be gained by denying self: doing such things as abstaining from sexual union and observing regulations. Martyrdom was prized. Others, in sharp contrast, concluded that since they were now predominantly spiritual by nature, they could not be corrupted. Their flesh could indulge in pagan festivals, gladiatorial contests, and promiscuous sex without contamination to their spirits.

The Apostle John's first letter is really a rebuttal against the ideas that eventually formed Gnosticism. He wrote, "That which . . . we have heard, which we have seen with our eyes, which we have looked at and our hands have touched—this we proclaim."[6] And, "Every spirit that acknowledges that Jesus Christ has come in the flesh is from God."[7]

As the church moved into the second century, it had to deal not only with enemies from without, but also with the variety of dissonant voices that had grown up within. A canon of New Testament writings had not yet been established; there was no commonly held set of beliefs. The primary sects were Ebionism, Marcionism, Montanism, and Donatism. Some of these sects were clearly heretical. The Marcionites, for example, taught that the Old Testament held no authority for Christians, that the God of the Old Testament and of the New Testament are two distinct deities. They held that the Old Testament Jewish God was evil. A world that contained suffering and cruelty must be, they thought, the work of an evil being, and not of a good God. They concluded that a second god had hidden himself, making his first appearance as Christ.

What were the defenses against all of these false teachings? One early bulwark was found in the creeds. As the creeds were developed, they served as a plumb line that measured truth against error. The earliest of these, the Apostles' Creed, is of uncertain origin, but it is believed to come from the oral teachings of the apostles and was in common use by the middle of the second century as a confession at baptism. The statement embraced the nature of God, of Jesus Christ, and the essential truths that comprise the gospel.

The Nicene Creed deals with questions concerning the nature of the Incarnation, and was initially drafted at the Council of Nicaea in AD 325. The phrase "being of one substance with the Father," a part of the creed, reveals the issue that was at stake.

With our reliance on the Scriptures today, these creeds and their successors seem unimportant to many of us. But their role in the history of God's people cannot be underestimated.

The other major attempt to deal with error and to preserve unity was to strengthen the authority and organization of the church. That is the topic of the rest of this chapter.

WHAT WOULD YOU HAVE DONE?

This brief description of the social and cultural context of the second century helps us understand something of what the church had to deal with. As we saw, Christianity was a maligned sect with beliefs that were deemed foolish and dangerous. It was persecuted from without, and torn by factions within. What was to keep everyone from being reabsorbed back into the bloodstream of Greek culture? Under the circumstances, what would you have done?

It is easy to judge the past, as things always seem so clear in retrospect. One look at the present, however, should be sufficient to cure us of whatever arrogance we might possess. We presently struggle to make wise decisions in the midst of today's myriad of issues. So did those involved in the formation of the church in those first centuries.

THE CHURCH FATHERS AND APOLOGISTS: WHAT THEY DID

It seems to me the measures taken to preserve the gospel and to protect the unity of the church in the formative period between the death of the last of the original twelve and the year 400 can be summarized in the works of four men. They are Ignatius, Irenaeus, Cyprian, and Augustine. Others could and probably should be mentioned, but these four, I feel, are adequate to carry the story. Our interest here is not just to understand what each of these men said and did, but to assess the effects of their work upon the church's ability to go to the world.

Ignatius: Bishop of Antioch

Ignatius, bishop of Antioch, was one of the Church Fathers—the name given to the writers of Christian literature who immediately succeeded the Twelve (AD 95–150).

Prior to the Church Fathers, the Christian community had no system of centralized administration. But early in the second century the beginnings of a central structure appeared. "The first epistle of Clement stressed the importance of 'decency and order' in the Church. And part of this order was a hierarchical structure. Women were to be subject to men, the young to the old, the 'multitude' to the presbyters, or alternatively to bishops and deacons selected for this purpose."[8]

By the time Ignatius did his writing, perhaps twenty years later, he was able to define the system in very clear terms. Ignatius was condemned to be cast to the beasts in the Roman amphitheater in about 117. While on his way to martyrdom he wrote seven letters. In one, addressed to the Smyrnaeans, he wrote, "Let all things therefore be done by you with good order in Christ. Let the laity be subject to the deacons; the deacons to the presbyters; the presbyters to the bishop; the bishop to Christ, even as He is to the Father."[9]

Ignatius commanded that presbyters and deacons be heeded as the recognized officers in the church. He also held that nothing was to be done without the bishop, that a baptism or the celebration of a love feast was unlawful without the bishop. The Eucharist could only be administered either by the bishop himself or by someone designated by him.

At the time of Ignatius each flock was independent, but eventually the system of bishops expanded from a bishop over each local body, to a bishop over each city, to a college of bishops, to a monarchical ruling body.

The intentions of the Church Fathers seem clear. They were concerned about unity and order within the church, and were looking for a system of defense against heresy from without. They achieved their goals, but at an awful price. They created a clergy-laity caste system, which put the average believer out of business in terms of his or her ministry in the gospel. The freedom experienced in the New Testament period vanished as the authority of the bishops grew. We will see how this progresses as we turn now to Irenaeus.

Irenaeus: c. AD 130–212

Irenaeus lived in the period of the apologists (AD 150–300). These writers contended for Christianity, combated paganism, and laid the beginnings of systematic theology. Irenaeus was raised in Smyrna and served as bishop of Lyons, in southern France, during 178–202. He was martyred in the persecution of Septimus Severus.

At this point in history, the churches had adopted an informal hierarchy consisting of small country churches, city churches, capital city churches, and major city churches. There were major city churches in Jerusalem, Antioch, Alexandria, Constantinople, and Rome.

Irenaeus, distressed by what he regarded as errors and corruptions of the gospel, wrote an extensive treatise called *Against Heresies*. In this treatise he emphasized the importance of the organic unity of the church; that this organic unity, as described in the Bible, should find visible expression in a political unity. This political unity was to be achieved and maintained by a perpetual succession of bishops from Christ. He insisted that the apostles had transmitted faithfully and accurately what had been taught them by Christ, and that they had appointed as successors bishops to whom they had committed the churches. In so doing they had undoubtedly also passed on to them the truth Christ had entrusted to them.

In his treatise Irenaeus wrote, "We do put to confusion all those who . . . assemble in unauthorized meetings . . . by indicating that tradition derived from the apostles . . . and organized at Rome by the two most glorious apostles, Peter and Paul, . . . which comes down to our time by means of the successions of the bishops. For it is a matter of necessity that every Church should agree with this Church, on account of its preeminent authority."[10]

Notice how Irenaeus shifted paradigms, from church as community to church as institution. A colleague of mine refers to this shift as a "hinge of history." David Bosch, speaking of this shift in the church, said, "Its white-hot convictions, poured into the hearts of the first adherents, cooled down and became crystallized codes, solidified institutions and petrified dogmas. The prophet became a priest of the establishment, charisma became office, and love became routine. The horizon was no longer the world but the boundaries of the local parish."[11]

Once again we see how, out of a legitimate concern for the purity of the gospel and for the unity of the body, measures were taken that had negative countereffects. Even a spontaneous neighborhood Bible study could now be ruled unlawful. It could be shut down by the single question, Have you been authorized by the bishop to be doing this?

Cyprian: Bishop of Carthage and Third-Century Martyr

We saw in the previous chapter how, in the first century, every Christian was held to be a priest unto God, serving God's people and the unbeliever, but by the end of the second century the clergy had been established as a separate "order" that assumed virtually exclusive rights to the ministry. As the clerical hierarchy refined its institutions, the average believer was, accordingly, deprived of the little that remained in his field of service. Cyprian stands out as another who contributed to this process.

The church continued to be plagued by persecution from without and schism from within. Cyprian, like those who went before him, believed that the solutions lay in the institutionalization of the church. In his treatise, *The Unity of the Church*, he developed the idea of unbroken, apostolic succession beginning with Peter. This concept of succession allowed Cyprian and others to challenge anyone outside the institution with the command, "Produce the origin of your churches; display the order of your bishops."[12] Whoever could not comply was declared a heretic.

Thus, in Cyprian's mind, the system of bishops represented the whole church. He said, "Whence you ought to know that the bishop is in the Church, and the Church is in the bishop; and if anyone be not with the bishop, that he is not in the Church. . . . The Church, which is Catholic and one, is not cut or divided, but is indeed connected and bound together by the cement of priests who cohere with one another."[13]

The next step in the progression follows inevitably. Cyprian would naturally conclude there could be no salvation outside the institution. He wrote, "You cannot have God for your father unless you have the Church for your mother."[14] Ironically, the final effect of his efforts was the distortion of the very gospel he gave his life to preserve!

Paul Johnson summarizes the results of this period in this way: "Law implied obedience; and obedience implied authority. What was this authority? The Church. What constituted the Church? *The men who ran it.* . . . Who was in charge of the process [of explaining Scripture]? The Church. What was the Church? *The men who ran it.*"[15] We will look now at the next logical step led by Augustine, the joining of this authoritarian church with the power of the state.

Augustine: Bishop of Hippo (AD 354–431)

In Augustine's time, the fortunes of the church in relation to the state had begun to change. An alliance with the empire began with Constantine. So the church found itself busy coming to terms with the world from which it had, to that point, stood apart. Augustine, in his widely read *City of God*, provided a philosophical basis that not only served the occasion but has affected the Christian faith until today.

Let us take a look at Kenneth Latourette's description of Augustine's theology and at Paul Johnson's description of the effects.

> Augustine, in accordance with the Biblical view, maintained that it [history] had a beginning and a culmination. . . . Augustine regarded the passing of the Empire with confident hope, believing that the Roman realm was to be replaced by an infinitely better order, that to be established by God. Augustine held that from the time of man's first rebellion against God two cities, the earthly and heavenly, had existed . . . The earthly was formed by love of self and pride. It was not entirely bad, for Babylon and Rome, its highest representatives, and the other governments had, out of regard for self-interest, brought peace and order. The heavenly city, on the other hand, is dominated "by the love of God even to the contempt of self." Men enter it here and now and it is represented by the Church, although not all in the Church are its citizens. . . . all history has been directed and governed by God and moves to a climax in a society in which God's will is perfectly to be accomplished.[16]

> It is clear that the church was the product of the Gospel. It is also clear that the visible, institutionalized church, whether Catholic or one of the bodies which dissented, was shot through and through with contradictions to the Gospel. As Augustine frankly recognized, the two cities, the

earthly and the heavenly, are intermingled. He held that they are to continue to be entangled until the last judgement effects their separation.[17]

Christianity was not the anti-society—it was society. Led by the elect, its duty was to transform, absorb and perfect all existing bonds of human relations, all human activities and institutions, to regularize and codify and elevate every aspect of life. Here was the germ of the medieval idea of a total society.[18]

It was at this point that Augustine's ideas began to be applied in some very negative ways.

The idea of a total Christian society necessarily included the idea of a compulsory society. People could not choose to belong or not belong. . . . Augustine did not shrink from the logic of his position. Indeed, to the problem of coercing the Donatists he brought . . . the willingness to use violence in a spiritual cause. . . . Why not? he would ask. If the State used such methods [torture] for its own miserable purposes, was not the Church entitled to do the same and more for its own far greater ones? He not only accepted, he became the theorist of, persecution. . . . And then, this was Christ's own way. Had not he, "by great violence," "coerced" Paul into Christianity? Was not this the meaning of the text from Luke 14:23: "Compel them to come in"?[19]

Thus, according to Augustine, the state needed the church to transform society, and the church needed the state to enforce that transformation. That was a fearsome arrangement. Nonetheless, it endured over the next thousand years as the foundational concept of the Middle Ages, a period often characterized by despondent passivity. Consumed with anxiety over their eternal destinies, and believing that the church held control over them, people resigned themselves to awaiting their fate.

Augustine's influence on the church is significant to our

discussion in that his idea of Christianity as a powerful, physical, and institutional presence in the world eventually resulted in papal supremacy. The concept of a universal church, which began with Ignatius, was advocated by Irenaeus, and more clearly defined by Cyprian, was fully articulated by Augustine.

Augustine believed that the visible institution of the Catholic church throughout the world was the Body of Christ, and that outside it there was no salvation. He also thought both baptism and the Lord's Supper were necessary for salvation, but that these did not guarantee one was among God's elect. As long as a person is in this mortal flesh, according to Augustine, that person shall be uncertain where he or she is in the number of the predestined.[20]

Supported by Augustinian theology, the clergy exerted unbelievable power throughout the Middle Ages. Heaven and hell were in their hands. Thus, not only had the average believer forfeited ministry to the clergy, but access to personal salvation was in the hands of the clergy as well. The possibility that God's people might function according to our thesis had been destroyed. The average believer was encircled by the institutional church.

WHAT SHOULD THEY HAVE DONE?

All of these men we have just described were both brilliant and godly. They were zealous to the point of death for the purity of the gospel and for the unity of God's people. We are indebted to them, for they did much to preserve the faith we now enjoy. Yet, as we have seen, there were seeds of death in the ideas they put into motion, and eventually these ideas destroyed the very things they were laboring to preserve. This frightens me. Sincerity and zeal do not serve as guarantees against error. It is probably true that anything that has human fingerprints on it is seriously marred and will eventually need replacing by God, the Lord of His people. Even our best ideas, in time, result in unintended consequences.

But what can we conclude? With the advantage of hindsight let us ask the question, What should they have done? Does the Bible give us anything to go on in this matter? There are lessons to be learned from both Jesus and the Apostle Paul.

Lessons from Jesus

As Jesus looked to the future, He knew what He was sending His followers into. He warned them, "You will be handed over to be persecuted and put to death, and you will be hated by all nations because of me. . . . Many will turn away from the faith . . . many false prophets will appear and deceive many people."[21] But Jesus coped with these pressures in ways very different from the ones we just observed.

Calling on His Father to protect His people, He said, "Holy Father, protect them by the power of your name . . . so that they may be one as we are one. While I was with them, I protected them and kept them safe by that name you gave me. . . . My prayer is not that you take them out of the world but that you protect them from the evil one. . . . As you sent me into the world, I have sent them into the world."[22] Jesus never said or did anything to indicate that structure and organization could serve to protect God's people. Shepherds and servants, yes, they would be needed, but He never talked about structure. Not that He was against structure. It is necessary, as we shall see, but for protecting His people, He had something far more trustworthy—the Holy Spirit. As He was about to return to His Father, He told His disciples, "Do not leave Jerusalem, but wait for the gift my Father promised . . . the Holy Spirit."[23] He would teach them all things. He would keep them and empower them.

Lessons from Paul

In Acts 20, we find the Apostle Paul preparing to depart from Ephesus, where he had devoted three-and-a-half years to establishing the believers. In his final conversation with the leaders, he reminded them of the responsibility of shepherding God's people. He acknowledged the inevitable dangers of division and false teaching. But he did not attempt to institute a protective organization. Instead he said, "I commit you to God and to the word of his grace."[24] Those struggling believers were surrounded by dangers of every sort, but Paul believed there was more strength to be found in the Spirit of God and the Word of God than there was in institutional structures. The Church Fathers we just reviewed either did not possess this same insight, or they did not have the courage to take the risk of letting Christ preserve His people.

I am not saying that organizations and institutions are wrong. Life would be maddeningly chaotic without them, but they are often misused. I believe that what we saw in our review represents a misuse. To begin with, these men took their cues for organizing and administrating the church from the model of the Roman Empire rather than from Christ and the Scriptures. But their more serious error lies in the fact that they counted on the structures they had created to preserve the saints and their faith. As a result, "Christianity had become in many striking ways a mirror-image of the empire itself. It was catholic, universal, ecumenical, orderly, international, multi-racial and increasingly legalistic. It was administered by a professional class of literates who in some ways functioned like bureaucrats and its bishops, like imperial governors, legates or prefects, had wide discretionary powers to interpret the law."[25]

I cannot but wonder what would have come of God's people had they continued to count on the Holy Spirit, rather than on structures, for their survival. And what would we be today had they maintained a more balanced focus, concerning themselves with the importance of every believer being involved in the life of the body and its mission in society, along with its concerns for purity of doctrine and organizational unity? Certain things would be very different today had they maintained that balance. And who knows how deeply the gospel would have penetrated into society!

FROM THE MEDIEVAL CHURCH
TO THE REFORMATION: 600–1517

In this section we will span almost a millennium with just a few short paragraphs. The course for the church of the Middle Ages had been set by the year 600, so our attention will be directed more toward the forces that eventually brought about the Reformation.

In treating the Middle Ages in this way, I could contribute to the popular notion that the Middle Ages was a period in history where nothing really happened, and what did happen was bad.

That is not true. Many great things happened, but this is not a book of complete history.

The glimpses we get of some early popes reveal that the papal structure, once conceived, quickly became a powerful institution. They also reveal that those popes, and the churches under their authority, made some amazing contributions to society, and to the expansion of the gospel.

Paul Johnson describes the varied activities of an early Dark Age pope.[26] Gregory I, who assumed the papacy in 589, occupied himself with a variety of business and social matters. He repaired aqueducts, bred horses, slaughtered cattle, administered legacies, set the price levels on rents and leases, and so on. Motivated by the need to build a financial base for the ecclesiastical administration, Gregory I fixed taxes on marriages, death duties, and land.

The clergy under Gregory I already had a caste structure that was reflected in their dress. Both the structure and the attitude mirrored the imperial senate and legislature. So, in effect, the clergy was imitating imperial Rome in appearance as well as function.

The clergy's great contribution to this period was the concept and application of law. The early Dark Age church had a complete and sophisticated body of written law, which it transmitted via missionary bishops to the barbarian world. When the barbarian societies accepted baptism, the bishops almost immediately set up arrangements to link the legal customs of the church with the existing pagan law codes. Thus the church became identified with progress and the future in the minds of the barbarians. Christianization was seen to be the point at which a people passed from being primitive and barbarous to civilized. The church gave barbarian society institutions, law, and history. It also introduced superior economic and agricultural techniques, as the monks who scattered out over Europe proved to be good farmers.

It was inevitable, given the theology, institution, and industry of the church of the Middle Ages, that it would increasingly accumulate power. That power, in turn, invited abuse. Pope Innocent III (r. 1198–1216) consolidated that power in what amounted to a theory of papal world government. The universal church, he wrote, exercised plenary powers in all aspects of government. He said, "By me kings reign and princes decree justice."[27] With this, Innocent III challenged the office of the emperor itself. "Either the Pope was the emperor's chief bishop; or the emperor was the Pope's nominee and puppet."[28] One or the other had to go. This launched a ferocious power struggle that eventually demanded the Reformation.

The papal weapons in this struggle were excommunication and interdict. These were terrifying weapons, as excommunication was thought to sentence a person to eternal doom, and interdict meant the priests would go on strike, refusing to perform marriages, burials, etc. As the power struggle accelerated, the bishops increasingly abused these weapons. Antagonism between king and clergy could only grow.

In this period, there were kings who clung to the ideal of a single Christian church and state. England's Henry II was one of these. He genuinely wanted to make the Christian society work. He believed that an active, vigorous, even militant church was necessary for the well-being of the commonwealth. But by his time, in the twelfth century, the posture of the papacy had become so radical that this good will was wasted. The forerunners of the Reformation soon began to make themselves heard.

THE EARLY REFORMERS

Reviewing the issues raised by the early reformers reveals the forces that drove the Reformation itself.

Peter Waldo: d.c. 1217

Among the earliest harbingers of the Reformation was Peter Waldo, a wealthy merchant of Lyons. Seeking to imitate Christ, he sold everything and went out to preach in city and countryside. He soon attracted followers who did the same. The church forbade them, and in 1184 Waldo was excommunicated by the pope. Nonetheless they continued.

Waldo preached against corruption in the church. He held that women and laymen could preach, that masses and prayers for the dead were without value, and that a layperson was as competent as a priest to hear confessions.

Waldo and his followers, the Waldenses, were branded as heretics. The Catholic Church and the civil authorities set out to eliminate them. They were persecuted until few survived.

John Wyclif: c. 1328–84

John Wyclif was a student and teacher at Oxford. He attacked the papacy with the charge that popes can and do make mistakes, and that a worldly pope was subject to discipline and should be removed from office. He maintained that "salvation does not depend upon a connection with the visible Church or upon the mediation of the priesthood, but solely upon election by God."[29] He condemned the worship of saints and relics, and pilgrimages. He rejected the idea of indulgences and masses for the dead.

His most audacious move was to translate the Bible from the Vulgate into the English vernacular. He insisted that the Scriptures were the supreme authority, and that ordinary people could understand them. He sent out traveling preachers whom he called "poor priests that preach . . . unlearned and simple" men, or simply "itinerant preachers." They preached wherever they could get a hearing—on the roads, in villages, or church yards.

Through his writings and the labors of the itinerants, Wyclif won a large number of followers, known as Lollards.

John Hus: c. 1373–1415

Hus, stimulated by Wyclif's writings, denounced the evils in the Bohemian Catholic Church and society. He charged the clergy, from the parish priest to the pope, with corruption. He held that Christ, not Peter, was the Head of the church, and that the Bible was the sole rule for life.

Hus's primary concern was moral reform. He called for a moral clergy and free preaching of the gospel. Hus was condemned for his beliefs and burned at the stake on July 6, 1415.

Erasmus: c. 1466–1536

In 1499 Erasmus heard the dean of Saint Paul's, John Colet, lecture at Oxford, England, on the book of Romans. This so inspired Erasmus that he devoted the next forty years of his life to reexamining the Scriptures, and to writing an array of small, inexpensive books for wide distribution.

Erasmus regarded himself as a layman. He supported himself with his publications and insisted that there could be no intermediaries between Christians and the Scriptures. He wanted to see the Bible as accessible as possible—and in vernacular translations. This was a bold position, because from about AD 1080 the clergy totally forbade laymen from reading the Bible—whether vernacular or not. Attempts to examine the Bible were viewed as proof of heresy and could cost one his or her life!

Summary

Certain recurring themes are apparent in the positions of the early reformers. They protested against the corruption of the clergy, right up to the papacy. They questioned the very concept of a papacy. They called for free access to the Scriptures for lay people, and defended their rights to preach and to minister. Thus, in Latourette's words, "The ground swell issuing from the rank and file of Christians was to come to flood tide." It would purify the Roman Catholic Church of some of its worst moral abuses, and would flow into "one or another aspect of what is collectively known as Protestantism."[30]

But would these fresh winds that were blowing across the church be strong enough to bring the ideals of our thesis back to where they could be practiced?

FROM THE REFORMATION TO THE PURITANS: 1517–1628

The Reformation was not a single movement as some might think. It was more like a convoy of movements that proceeded simultaneously. The Protestant Reformation consisted of four primary movements: Lutheran, Reformed, Anabaptist, and Anglican. The Catholic Reformation came as a response to these, and was really a counterreformation. Both Catholic and Protestant movements had in common the desire to cleanse the church of corruption and correct its errors.

In this section we will try to understand how the Reformation influenced the church's perception of its responsibility to the unbelieving world, and its view of the average believer's ministry inside and outside the church. Each of the Protestant movements handled this question somewhat differently.

Lutheranism

Martin Luther (1483–1546) was the first outstanding leader of Protestantism. While a monk, the meaning of the phrase in Romans 1:17, "The just shall live by faith," dawned on him. From that time on (about 1516), Luther lived in awe of God's forgiveness and the free gift of salvation. Through Luther, "justification by faith" became the dominant truth.

The issuance of indulgences by the Roman Catholic Church was based on the belief that the pope could draw on the treasury of the saints to remit the temporal penalties for sin for both the living and the souls in purgatory. The indulgence was a very marketable idea. Its lucrative potential invited clerical corruption. Thus, the sale of indulgences did much to prompt the Reformation: it provoked Luther, on October 31, 1517, to post his ninety-five theses on the door of the Castle Church in Wittenberg, Germany. Luther was throwing down the gauntlet, offering to debate the subject with anyone disposed to take him on. That act is commonly viewed as the beginning of the Reformation.

Luther took issue with the idea that one could amass good works by going on pilgrimages, fasting, confessing, and calling on the saints. He rejected the notion that popes, bishops, priests, and monks were superior to the laity. All Christians, he maintained, were consecrated priests and thereby competent to discern what was right in matters of faith. He held that each Christian had the right and duty to interpret the Scriptures, the sole authority.

In April 1521, Luther defended himself before the judiciary body of the church and the emperor. Given the mood of the day, and what had happened to Hus under similar circumstances, one wonders how he lived to tell about it. "A single individual was pitting his reason and his integrity against established institutions which were the bulwark of society."[31]

Luther started a movement and subsequently organized it. He viewed the church as "the assembly of all the believers in Christ upon earth . . . though they be a thousand miles apart in body, yet they are called an assembly in spirit because each one preaches, believes, hopes, loves, and lives like the other. . . . And this unity is of itself sufficient to make a Church."[32]

In defining the visible church Luther said, "The external marks, whereby one can perceive where this Church is on earth, are baptism, the Sacrament and the Gospel; and not Rome, or this place, or that. For where baptism and the Gospel are, no one may doubt that there are saints, even if it were only the babes in their cradles."[33]

The Reformed Churches

Although the Reformed movement within Protestantism came about through the efforts of several people, John Calvin (1509–64) did the most to shape it. At twenty-six years of age, in Basel, Switzerland, Calvin published his first edition of *The Institutes of the Christian Religion.* This is probably the single most influential book of the Protestant Reformation because it offered a clear, orderly, comprehensive presentation of the Christian faith. Calvin revised this work throughout his lifetime, publishing his fourth revision in 1559.

In addressing the subject of the church, Calvin maintained that it was not identical with any visible institution, but included all the elect. It was invisible and known only to God. As to the visible manifestation of the church, he said it existed "wherever we find the word of God purely preached and heard, and the sacraments administered according to the institution of Christ." Church members included "all those who by a confession of faith, an exemplary life, and a participation of the sacraments profess the same God and Christ as ourselves."[34]

Calvin was concerned that there be order in the church. The church should have judiciaries appointed to censure vice and to excommunicate wayward parishioners. Calvin held that originally there were apostles, prophets, evangelists, pastors, and teachers. He believed God raised up the first three only for special occasions, while pastors and teachers were constant.

Calvin held to the view, inspired by Augustine, of a holy community where church and state functioned together. He attempted to make the city of Geneva a model of this cooperation.

The Anabaptists

The Anabaptist Movement was contemporaneous with Lutheranism and Calvinism, but it was more radical than either. Its origins are uncertain. It was not led by a few strong individuals in the way the Lutheran and Reformed movements were. Consequently, considerable diversity makes it difficult to summarize what Anabaptists believed.

In general, they looked to the Scriptures and especially the New Testament as their authority. They wished to return to first-century primitive Christianity, and tended to withdraw from society, to seek perfection in communities of their own—far from the contamination of the world. They believed in churches composed of those who had experienced new birth. They rejected infant baptism, regarding as valid only the baptism administered to conscious believers. This is where they got their name. It was a nickname that stuck—Anabaptist, those who baptize a second time.

Among the strands of Anabaptists were some who believed that in them prophecy had been revived. Some denied the divinity of Christ. Many were ardently missionary, seeking to persuade not only Christians of their views, but also of carrying the gospel to all mankind.

The Anabaptists were persecuted from every side: by the Roman Catholic Church, by the Lutherans, and by the Reformed Church.

The Anglicans and the Puritans

First encouraged for political and personal reasons by Henry VIII, the Anglican Reformation in England was different from the others. In order to get a divorce from Katherine of Aragon, and the right to marry Anne Boleyn, he had to gain control of the Roman Catholic Church in England. The Act of Supremacy, issued in 1534, achieved that end. It declared the king as "the only supreme head in earth of the Church of England." In doctrine, the Church of England remained basically unchanged. One difference, of course, was in its definition of the church. According to the Anglican creed, "The visible Church of Christ is the congregation of faithful men in which the pure Word of God is preached, and the sacraments be duly administered according to Christ's ordinance in all those things that of necessity are requisite to the same."[35]

The Puritans, a party within the Anglican Church, wanted further reform. Their objectives were to purify the church according to the Bible, to restrict church membership to those who had demonstrated their election, and to establish the autonomy of particular congregations.

In 1628 more than twenty thousand Puritans embarked for New England to work out the complete reformation, which they felt had not yet been accomplished in England and Europe.

HOW DID IT GO WITH THE PURITANS?

The migration of the Puritans began in 1628 and lasted sixteen years. The motivating force behind those life-threatening, one-way journeys was the covenant these Puritans had made with God and with one another to be a church and a society that was Christian in the way they defined it. "They saw their task of settlement as God-given: an 'errand into the wilderness,' an experiment in Christian living, the founding of a 'city upon a hill.'"[36]

Peter Marshall and David Manuel write of the structure of Puritan life. As the Puritans settled, "First a church covenanted together, *then* the town formed around it."[37] Thus for them church and government were inseparable. Life revolved around the church.

> Sunday was the *first* day of the week, not the last. There was the morning service, which lasted three to four hours, after which they adjourned for a light lunch and returned for the afternoon teaching which could run another three hours. Then came Sunday dinner, the hardiest meal of the week.[38]

The pastor was the key figure, generally a graduate of Oxford or Cambridge. As the best educated man in the community, he was the sole source of both secular and religious knowledge. Thus, he served multiple needs; he pastored, he educated. He served as the equivalent of our anchorman on the daily news.

The Puritans, and the early American settlers of other ecclesiastical origins, such as the Pilgrims, demonstrated great spiritual vitality. Personal holiness and integrity were life-and-death issues. They were a disciplined people and imposed their norms on one another.

As for church structure, the early settlers did break away from the clerical hierarchies common to Europe, with congregationalism becoming the common replacement. But the pastor and the sermon continued to be the centerpiece of church life. It's hard to conceive how it could have been any different, as the society was predominantly rural, and illiteracy was high.

We are indebted to the Puritans for what they brought to the founding of our nation. The biblical religion of those first American settlers had significant influence on the legal, political, and economic systems of the fledgling nation. They helped lay the moral foundations upon which this nation has stood.

But the areas of our concern were not on their agenda.

WHAT HAPPENED—WHAT DIDN'T HAPPEN?

The more one reflects on the Reformation and on the achievements of those who made it happen, the more unbelievable it becomes. Again and again lone individuals, because of their convictions, defied and often confronted formidable institutions that held the power of life or death over them. Entire communities of unnamed believers accepted persecution, torture, and death in preference to denying what they believed. Certainly the signature of the Holy Spirit is written across that one-hundred-year period of our history. What would have come of the church had these people not done what they did? The issues they fought for were vital: justification by faith, the authority of the Scriptures and free access to them, the priesthood of the believer, and the call to purity and integrity.

But the question remains, Did the Reformation succeed in restoring the biblical perspective of the church as being God's people, sent into the world as witnesses? Did it restore to the believer his or her place in the ministry? Our answers are found in the work the Reformers did in redefining the church.

WHAT IS THE CHURCH, ACCORDING TO THE REFORMERS?

In this chapter we have looked at some of the Reformers' definitions of the church. When they repudiated the papal system, their previously held doctrine of the church fell apart. To that point, the pope had been the unifying factor for the church. His clerical hierarchy encompassed it. The Reformers had to set to the task of disentangling the church from the papacy. How, they had to ask themselves, should a church without a pope look? Most of them defined the church in two dimensions. That is, they described a universal, invisible church consisting of all who truly belonged to God, and they described its visible, local expression.

When we compare this two-dimensional definition with the multiform expression of God's people in the New Testament, it's hard not to conclude that something big is missing in their work. The church they describe seems to congregate more than anything else. The "traveling expressions" of God's people are absent. And although average believers gained the freedom to find salvation and study the Scriptures on their own, they did not recover their share of ownership in the ministry.

Three of the four Protestant Reformation movements—Lutheranism, Reformed Presbyterian, and Anglican—became state churches. Lutheranism and the Reformed Presbyterian Churches were, in many ways, a continuation of the Catholic Church in their respective lands. The same could be said for Anglicanism. Each sought to be the church of the entire community. They succeeded in several countries. People entered the church by infant baptism, and all people had their children baptized.

Thus, in the areas of our concern, nothing really changed. The clergy retained ownership of the ministry, and the "unbelieving world" was enrolled in the church. The Anabaptists were at the other extreme, as their posture was frequently separatist, avoiding contact with the unbelieving society.

Why could something so central as God's purpose for His people in the world and the nature of their ministry be missed in this historic period? I think it is because reforms are always in response to specific needs. They happen in a context. The Reformers dealt with the immediate needs as they perceived them. Without question, they changed the map in favor of the gospel. But they did not, could not, address every issue.

Most of the issues left unaddressed were pre-Roman Catholic Church in origin. They date back to the Church Fathers! The Reformers did not go so far as to question the precedents established by the Church Fathers prior to the Roman Catholic Church. The Church Fathers were the originators of the dichotomy between the clergy and the laity. True, the Protestant Reformers affirmed the priesthood of all believers, but they did little to facilitate their reinstatement into ministry on the levels called for by our thesis.

CHAPTER SIX

The Church in America

▼

We now proceed into the present in our tour through history in search of how the people of God have fared in discharging their ministry to the unbelieving world. In chapter 4 we saw how, even for that first generation, accomplishing those ideals was a delicate matter requiring voluntary, mutual submission between the apostles and elders who led the people of God. In the centuries immediately following, the freedom of the first century was lost to a hierarchical, controlling structure. This split the church into two castes—clergy and laity—and gave the clergy exclusive control over the ministry. As for the lost, they were incorporated into the church through compulsory baptism.

The Protestant Reformation didn't really fix this situation. It affirmed the truth that the Holy Spirit indwells and gifts every believer for service—the priesthood of every believer. But as Howard Snyder indicates, "Today, four centuries after the Reformation, the full implications of this Protestant affirmation have yet to be worked out." The dichotomy between clergy and laity persists. Snyder continues, "Because we repeatedly read this dichotomy into the Bible, it has become for us a great obstacle to a biblical understanding of the Church. Some fundamental rethinking is overdue precisely at this point."[1]

IN THE SHADOW OF THE PAST

In seventeenth-century America, life was rural and community-centered. The church and the town hall were close to each other in more ways than one. The church depended on the sermon and the sanctuary as the primary forms to accomplish its ministry. This served people well. Now however, at the end of the twentieth century, times have changed beyond belief. We find ourselves in an urban, insular society where church and state are becoming increasingly opposed to each other, and where biblical and popular thought are becoming more and more at odds. The days when we could expect the world to come to us are over. Yet we try. In fact, that's where we expend most all of our energy—trying to get the world to come to us.

Several months ago I participated in a forum on reaching the unchurched together with a number of church leaders. I had missed the first day, and when I joined the group they were discussing church parking lots. Someone was describing a way to identify cars that had never shown up at the church before. The conversation moved on to the relationship between parking lot size and church growth. One participant told of a church that had painted a mural on the wall above its parking lot to attract people.

At the first break I asked a friend to review the previous day's discussions. I learned the discussions had focused on what the church could do to attract the unchurched. Apparently, the parking lot was as far away from the church building as the discussions were going to get. I realized that this group and I were operating on different assumptions. They assumed that with the right approach the unchurched can be *attracted* to attend the church program. Most of the men at the seminar were pastors of churches containing over one thousand people—a fact that served to support their assumption. My assumption, in contrast, is that while some will be attracted, most unbelievers won't. People can be attracted to a church by what it offers, but the problem lies in who those people usually turn out to be. The overwhelming majority are a part of that migratory flock of church-goers who always seem to be looking for a place to land where more is happening. Increase of this sort isn't church growth at all. It's just a reshuffling of the same fifty-two cards.

Some unchurched people can be attracted to the church. There are several very encouraging examples of this occurring in the country today. But I'm convinced that these will always be the relatively few. The mainstream unchurched American society, swept up in the tide of modernity described earlier in this book, will not be able to break out to come to us. What about them? Our persistent "come to us" mind-set suggests that we really believe that people who refuse to come in the front door are beyond the reach of Christ.

FROM MOM AND POP TO DEMOGRAPHIC ANALYSIS

I paid my way through college by working as a butcher. I worked in a little over-the-counter shop in downtown Minneapolis. The butcher shop shared the store space with a fruit-and-vegetable stand. This was in the late 1950s. One of my duties was the bookkeeping at the end of each day. Over the four years of my employment, I watched the gross sales drop to a third of what they had been when I started. A pattern became evident. The Red Owl food chain was busy opening supermarkets in the suburbs. We could not compete with the service they offered: one-stop shopping where the customer could purchase everything needed, once a week, with plenty of easy parking. Every time a new Red Owl store opened, our sales would show another drop. Butcher shops were becoming obsolete. Eventually we went out of business.

Things at church weren't a whole lot different. Pop preached and Mom played the piano and directed the choir at the same time. Mrs. Hanson was a piercing soprano and Mr. Ferris never quite hit the note, but we all overlooked it. Sermons tested everyone's endurance, but they did give us something to discuss over our Sunday noon pot roast and mashed potatoes. The attitude was one of benign tolerance, but the thought of leaving to find something more interesting seldom received serious consideration. That was our church, soprano and all.

The revolution of the 1960s hit the church, just as it did every other institution of our society. Pop's preaching and that off-key choir was clearly not going to reach the world. It wasn't even reaching us. Christian young people who wanted more flocked to what are commonly called parachurch groups. It was harvest time among a generation in turmoil. I remember wondering, as I watched the ebbing of the local churches, if the tide would ever come back in for them. For the parachurch groups, the method didn't seem to matter out there on the campuses, military bases, or even in the streets. You could do it all wrong and still get a response. By the end of the decade the seminaries began to fill with the fruit of these efforts.

Again in the 1970s, the fortunes of the church took another turn. By the middle of the decade many of those seminarians of parachurch origins had graduated and had gained enough experience in church leadership to know what they wanted. Their campus or street experiences had enlarged their vision. Many were innovative and highly gifted and had an appreciation for excellence. The 1970s saw the emergence of the superchurch.

In the 1980s yet a new model for a successful church emerged. It has been described as the "entrepreneurial" church. This, too, is a reflection of our times.

The inspiration for the entrepreneurial church is summarized by George Barna as follows: "The point is clear—the Church is not making inroads into the lives and hearts of people. My contention, based on careful study of data and the activities of American churches, is that the major problem plaguing the Church is its failure to embrace a marketing orientation in what has become a marketing-driven environment."[2]

This model requires a spectrum of specialized ministries. According to Leith Anderson, "More and more Americans are opting for 'full service churches' that can offer quality and variety in music, extensive youth programs, diverse educational opportunities, a counseling staff, support groups, singles' ministry, athletic activities, multiple Sunday morning services, a modern nursery, and . . . other services and programs."[3] Obviously, only a large organization is able to provide all this, so size is a requisite. I have heard these churches described as "spiritual shopping malls" containing an array of specialized ministries under a single roof.

The entrepreneurial church has brought a new vocabulary to the elders' meeting. One is likely to hear discussions on "who is the customer," "learning the market," and "cost-results." There is nothing ambiguous about the definition of success in this model. It thinks "bottom line," in quantifiable terms. Performance is evaluated against the numbers.

Peter Drucker, America's guru on management, uses the church to illustrate a lesson in marketing: Businesses must market to *all* potential customers, not just to *their* customers. His illustration of successful use of this principle is the concept of "pastoral" churches that have learned to exploit demographic changes as marketing opportunities. "Traditional churches and synagogues in the U.S. have been losing members steadily for 40 years," he reports.

> [People] were bored with traditional churches and increasingly stayed home. . . . [Leaders of the new] pastoral churches saw them as "potential customers." They asked what the customers need and want in a church. They focus, as a result, on the individual's spiritual wants; and on the individual's need for a freely chosen but close community. And they try to satisfy the desire of the affluent younger people to be put to work in the church and to hold responsible positions in its governance.
>
> Fifteen years ago there were few such churches around, and most were quite small. Today there are some 20,000 large, pastoral churches, each with a membership of 2,000 people or more—and some 5,000 of them have congregations in excess of 4,000 or 5,000.[4]

Drucker's main point is that those who should be customers but aren't are the critical group to watch. And it requires right marketing action to get them.

Although these mammoth churches are the prevailing models of success, a very small percentage of the churches in the country make it into that circle. Leith Anderson reports that "there are an estimated 375,000 churches in the United States, and most of them are small. Half . . . have 75 or less at worship on a typical Sunday morning. Most are surprisingly stable and indestructible," Anderson observes. "[They] would probably continue to meet even if the pastor died, the building burned, and the treasury went bust. They are built upon and held together by permanent family relationships."[5] So, big churches are not the whole story, but aspirations definitely tend in the direction of bigness.

WHAT TO MAKE OF IT

Who says it doesn't work to try to attract people to the church? It sounds as if we have it down to a science, and that we're seeing results like never before. But how we evaluate these things really depends on what we're looking for. It depends on the questions we are asking.

If our concern is to see the church respond to the demographic and sociological changes in our society in such a way that it manages to hold on to its people, then we have much reason to be encouraged by what we are seeing. The church is managing to retain its own and many who are about to wander off. This is no small accomplishment given the pressures this pluralistic society is bringing to bear on the Christian community.

This book started out with a description of a series of influences that will reshape America, and inevitably the church as well. We saw how it is becoming increasingly difficult for a family to hold together both relationally and economically. The pace of life has quickened. Mobility has become a way of life. The job markets that correspond with many careers force mobility. That mobility now seems to have found its way into every sector of life, as we readily move from city to city, house to house, job to job, and sometimes marriage to marriage.

There was a time when one found in a church a permanent home for better or worse. Now many churchgoers join one church for a period of time in their lives and then, as their interests and needs change, think nothing of moving to another.[6] If this mobility is truly a cultural trait, church leaders face one of two choices as they seek to deal with it. They can choose to fight it and lose. Or they can understand it and discover how to work with it.

We have described the church's efforts to reach out to this society. What it has succeeded in doing has been primarily to retain its own people. It has also attracted back some who were on the fringes, who share a church heritage but had become inactive. This is no small accomplishment. It has managed this, in part, by taking lessons from the marketplace. It has learned well enough for Drucker to use the church as an illustration for industry on how to respond to the times!

But in reality, with all these innovations, we have really only managed to hold onto what is already ours. The rest of this society is not reading our ads. We have not really mobilized ourselves to take the initiative and go to the world.

Before we proceed to explore what might constitute an initiative of this sort, some observations are in order concerning this current trend I've just described. There is a down side.

THE DOWN SIDE

In the course of history, the church has tended to pattern its leadership style after the predominant power structure of a society. That continues to be the rule today. We saw how the Church Fathers viewed the church as a kingdom and followed the model of the empire. It seemed to be a good idea at the time, and it "worked." But we saw the bad fruit born of this imitation. In the United States the predominant model is business. Our commitment to democracy is also reflected in our churches, but as we have seen, we are obviously taking our cues from business.

The proponents of this trend argue that the church *is* business, and needs to be treated as such. It is true that there is a business side to church affairs. There has been ever since Acts 6. But the business side cannot be the controlling factor. It is interesting that the New Testament utilizes such a variety of metaphors to describe the church—a body, a bride, a building, a family, a field, a flock, a house, and a temple. I think the Spirit of God did this to keep us from locking in on a single model. I fear that the American church has stepped outside the Bible to take on a model that will bear some pretty bad fruit.

Richard Halverson puts it this way: "It makes a difference *how one thinks about the church.* Thinking of it as an organization *dictates one way of going . . .* thinking of it as an organism demands a totally different *modus operandi.* When the organizational aspect is primary—*size of membership, building and budget are decisive . . .* and measurable. When its organic nature is primary—*quality of life, attitudes, relationships are decisive . . .* and they do not yield easily to measurement."[7]

Bottom-Line Thinking

When we embrace the business model, we are forced to define success numerically. We think cost-results, asking, what do we get for our money, for our effort?

But how does one measure yeast hidden in dough—or the growth of the mustard seed? How do we keep track of the seed sown in the field? How do we quantify spiritual service—by the hour? How do we evaluate time spent in prayer? True spiritual results are not only beyond our control, often we can't even see them, much less explain how they happen. Not only can we not measure the ministry quantitatively, we distort it when we try.

Recently I was consulting with an organization that ministers to troubled kids. After months of work we came back with our recommendations. I sensed resistance to the new ideas, and I knew why. They had been evaluating their ministry on a cost-results basis. To talk about it costing "a buck a kid" made awfully good promotional copy. What we were recommending would transform the results of that ministry, but they wouldn't be able to make that claim any longer.

Numerical evaluation of ministry eventually becomes manipulative. It may start out well, but when slump time comes, the temptation is to apply pressure to get people to perform according to our definition of success. When that happens, everything gets turned around. Those being ministered to end up serving the leaders in the accomplishment of their goals, because people are the bottom line in this "business."

I could fill pages with illustrations that support this. I watched the organization I'm with fall into this, and then get out. We had to. Our people tended to do only the measurable things, the things they would get credit for. They were neglecting the intangibles that are really the soul of ministry.

Competition

Another bad effect that comes out of the business model is competition. Competition is good for business, and sports are no fun without it, but it cripples the Body of Christ.

In a recent conversation with a friend of mine, I asked him how things were going in his church. I knew that the church had gone through some leadership changes and other destabilizing circumstances. He replied, "We're doing okay, but it's tough. The city won't allow us to build any more on this site, and there are other churches in town that are into major building projects. They are the ones that have the image of being where things are happening. We were the happening place in the late 1970s and early 1980s, but our image is fading. Our interior decoration is getting tacky, so we have to redecorate. That costs money. It's hard to compete. I know that sounds awful, but that's the way it is."

That *is* awful, but given the choices we have made for measuring success, it is also inevitable. If success is measured in attendance, budgets, and buildings, then a particular congregation can quickly find itself in competition with the other congregations in town. This is so incongruous in light of what the Scriptures have to say about the body! How can a particular fellowship feel good about the last one hundred new members when it knows that eighty-seven of them came from another church two miles away that is going through difficult times? The Apostle Paul writes, "If one part suffers, every part suffers with it."[8] We are called to "do nothing out of selfish ambition or vain conceit, but in humility consider others better than [ourselves]."[9]

As we observed, we are dealing with a mobile society. Consequently, who is there and what happens at 9:30 and 11:00 on Sunday morning doesn't always mean what it did a few years ago. Frequently churches interpret a rapid influx of several hundred people as being solid growth, and as a signal that it's time to build. So they spend millions. Shortly thereafter, their fortunes change as the flock moves on. The faithful remnant spends the succeeding years in a maintenance mode. Lyle Schaller, a parish consultant, says, "A lot of congregations are demoralized because their No. 1 job is to feed the white elephant."[10] The adventure is gone. Passive participation sets in and breeds mediocrity in individual lives. We need to be alert to these tendencies, or values, that are inherent to our "business model," and resist them. We need to take care to replace these values born of pragmatism with values born of God's Word, by His Spirit.

REGAINING OUR MOBILITY

Again, how we feel about how we're doing as a church depends on the questions we are asking. When we look at ourselves from the perspective of our thesis, we have to say that nothing has really changed. We still operate within the same paradigm as did the church when our society was rural and largely illiterate. Although today's society is urban and literate, and although the mainstream of the unchurched has already philosophically moved away, our paradigm is still "come to, and listen to." We are still sermon- and sanctuary-centered in our forms. Consequently, we continue to gather the people who are willing to make that first move, and we continue to miss the rest.

I recently spent several hours with a group of Christian high school students. We were discussing their frustrations in attempting to reach their classmates. They face a formidable challenge. We discussed the prevailing problems of the high school student world: drugs, alcohol, sexual abuse, violence, and suicide. Their great dilemma was that no plausible environment exists where those who might be responsive to Christ can get help. Their nonChristian friends need a place where they can go to get a better look that will not demean them in the eyes of their peers. Some of the Christians had tried the only thing they knew—taking their friends to their church youth group. But the disaster rate had been total. Obviously misfits, their friends would vanish for good.

Finally, one of the students in his frustration exclaimed, "Let's face it. To get to heaven in this country you have to be born white, Anglo-Saxon, middle class, and Protestant." An exaggeration, but he made his point. It is our move. If we are to get to mainstream, unchurched Americans, we must take the initiative and meet them on their turf. Why is this so difficult for us to understand?

THE UNFINISHED REFORMATION

One of our primary problems is that the Reformers, as we have seen, left us with definitions of the church that are basically two dimensional. They describe the church universal. And they give us definitions of a local church. That's about it. The sad reality is that going to the lost, living Christlike lives among them and revealing Christ to them, is not in our ecclesiology. The believer has not made a whole lot of progress toward regaining his or her place in the ministry. The church came out of the Reformation with no vision for the penetration of society by believers and no provision for the traveling, or mobile, expressions of the people of God.

Missing: Equipping the Believer for Ministry

The believer is strategically positioned inside the marketplace, the neighborhood, and the institutions of our society. He or she is at the scene of the disaster when it is happening, is there at the moment of opportunity, to embrace and serve people as the occasion arises. The believer is the key to penetrating our society.

The primary function of leadership should be to serve those believers by equipping them for ministry. They need resources, skills, and constant encouragement. They need to be released and affirmed as they scatter to fulfill their functions in the body and among their unbelieving friends. There's only one problem. Our leaders don't know how to do this. That brings us to the matter of regaining our ability to go.

Missing: The "Traveling" Functions of the Body

The body is not complete where the traveling, itinerant functions are not being exercised. Ephesians 4:11 says it takes all the functions — apostles, prophets, evangelists, pastors, and teachers — to equip the saints. When we try to do it with less, it just doesn't work. There are things that the pastor-teacher can't bring to the equation. In part, the laity is at a loss today because proper equipping is just not available to them.

The mobile, traveling parts of the body are not just for foreign missions, as we may think. A church never outgrows its need to be stirred toward greater vision and service. And it takes all these parts to provide the experience and skill believers need if they are to begin to germinate in their own field. These mobile people are also needed to lead in new plantings in the hard-to-reach spots of our own society.

The Reformation got us started. It gave us the freedom we enjoy today. It gave us back our Bible. But the Reformers themselves would not have wanted us to stop where we have. It remains for us to carry the process forward, restoring the multiform expression of the people of God seen in the New Testament.

VOICES OF LEADERSHIP

It appears that the Spirit of God is leading a number of people to think along lines similar to those I have been expressing. For example, Robert E. Slocum, in his book *Maximize Your Ministry*, says, "The . . . church will need to focus on decentralized teams of equipped laity as the church in the world instead of concentrating all activities on Sundays at the sanctuary."[11] He also says, "I believe the 'great, great' congregations of the high-tech age will not be judged on size, growth rate, or the number of spiritual all-stars on their payroll. The 'great, great' churches will be those that serve as training camps and base camps for lay men and women who hear Christ call them to climb their particular mountain and who respond to that call."[12]

Another outstanding little book on this subject is *Love, Acceptance & Forgiveness*, by Jerry Cook. He puts it this way: "It is not the pastor's job to meet everybody's need. . . . The pastor should be a facilitator. . . . Two things are necessary: people must be trained to use their own gifts in ministry; and the church must grant the people the right to minister in crisis situations on the spot."[13] He observes that in the prevailing concept of the church, the emphasis is "visibility, organization, program, and promotion. . . . The goals . . . are defined in terms of numbers in attendance, of budget and of facility. . . . [This is because,] if you are going to do a great work for God and it's all within the building, then you must have an enormous building."[14] And this requires, of course, a large, professionally trained staff.

CONCLUSION

So far, the innovations and changes we have made as a church have remained within our historical paradigm. We have yet to really question the assumptions that paradigm rests upon. I believe it is time for that, but this must be done with great care and with humility before God and one another. We must begin by asking the right questions.

The question we most ask is, "What's working that will increase our numbers?" We thus betray our pragmatism. "Good" is what "works." What we need to ask is, "What do the Scriptures have to say about ministry?" It is disturbingly rare to find people who seek to interpret the times and the role of God's people in our times from the context of biblical truth. We *can* do that—we have the people, the freedom, and the resources. And it is not really that difficult.

Our churches are rich in gifted, godly people who hunger to live out their commitment to Christ and His purposes. We have many gifted teachers, pastors, and administrators who excel in what they do, and who have demonstrated their skill with the Scriptures. Many of these people, both staff and members, live with vague feelings of dissatisfaction over what their Christian experience is offering them. Some attempt to live in two worlds, maintaining their church activities while trying at the same time to penetrate their circles with the gospel. They feel the tension from both sides. Others have resigned themselves to living with the status quo, having concluded that there are no real alternatives. Then there is a third category, the growing number who are just dropping out.

But the fact remains that there is an abundance of spiritually mature, easily motivated believers among God's people today.

Another great asset is the freedom we enjoy today as a church. The repressive insistence on conformity that controlled the church in previous centuries is gone. Today, we are free to think, to question, and to innovate. True, some of us have yet to discover that the door to the cage is open, but the freedom is there. The many exciting, innovative experiments already going on are testimony to that fact.

And we have the financial resources. *Fortune* magazine reports, "If U.S. religion were a company, it would be number 5 on the *Fortune 500*, its 500 billion of revenues putting it behind IBM and just ahead of G.E. Church land and buildings are worth uncounted billions . . . the figures don't include volunteer work, worth a jaw-dropping 75 billion a year."[15]

God's people today are gifted and wealthy, with seemingly limitless possibilities. Before God this adds up to an awesome responsibility! How do we discharge this responsibility constructively, in ways that put us where we belong, doing what we should be doing, and at the same time strengthening and affirming all that is good in the church as it is? The rest of this book will focus on how to achieve this ideal.

Part III
PATTERNS FOR THE FUTURE

CHAPTER SEVEN

Freedom and Diversity: A First-Century Example

▼

We concluded the last chapter with the observation that we, as a church, have developed our ability to retain our own, but we have not yet recovered our mobility to go to the unbelieving world. We have work to do. We need to discover how to go to our society in ways that realistically take the differences in thinking and values into account.

I find it fascinating that God's people in the first century faced a task not unlike what we are facing today. In fact, the challenges they faced were far more daunting than what we are dealing with. They were called upon to sort out Jesus from Judaism in order to become a people for all nations. We are called upon to sort out Jesus from our religious traditions in order to make Him available to our nation. In the first century they managed to make those changes without tearing themselves apart in the process. Perhaps, if we examine how they did it, we can do it too. That's what this chapter is all about.

In taking us to the New Testament to see how the early Christians dealt with the demand for diversity in their situation, I am not suggesting that what they did is normative for us. Those first Christians were by no means infallible. Much of what they did was done in response to immediate situations that demanded attention. For example, the reason the believers in Jerusalem appointed seven men to serve as deacons was because there was work for seven men to do. There were some Grecian widows who were neglected. They did what was natural, or obvious. In Jerusalem, the believers met in the Temple. The Temple was the customary place of prayer even before Christ came along. They found practical solutions to problems. In Ephesus, Paul evangelized and taught at the school of Tyrannus, probably because Tyrannus made it available to him after he was kicked out of the synagogue.

To insist on seven deacons, or on Temple worship, or to make a principle out of what happened in the school of Tyrannus, is to misapply the Scriptures. Not all of what happened among these first Christians was even right. They made mistakes. Paul and Barnabas fought with each other. Peter and Paul had their bad days with one another. So we do not want to recreate the first century. But the Holy Spirit did preserve the record of what they did for our instruction. As we succeed in understanding what they did and why they did it—and where we can verify that their actions were an outworking of biblical principles—we are rewarded with guidance that will serve us in our day. So, as we work our way through this chapter, our attention will be on the *function*, or action, that is being exercised rather than on the particular *form*, or structure, of their activities.

"TO THE JEW FIRST"

If we are to understand the tensions the early Christians had to work through, we need to appreciate something of what it meant to be a Jew in those days, especially one who had come to believe in Christ.

God gave the gospel to the Jew first. I find it fascinating that He orchestrated events so that the arrival of the Holy Spirit among those 120 disciples, waiting in a room in Jerusalem that Sunday morning, May 28, AD 30, coincided with the annual pilgrimage of devout Jews to that city. It was Pentecost, and "there were staying in Jerusalem God-fearing Jews from every nation under heaven." All Peter and the others had to do was explain what was going on, and three thousand people believed. With one event the news of

Christ eventually found its way back out to those nations.

In the first chapters of Acts the sermons were addressed to "men of Israel," to "brothers and fathers," and usually began with a recounting of familiar stories of Abraham, Isaac, and Jacob. Those first believers, all Jews, shared a world of common ground with the people of their nation, and they made the most of it. They soon filled Jerusalem with the news of the Resurrection. As we saw in chapter 4, it was persecution by their own people, not strategic planning, that got the people of God out of Jerusalem and into Judea and Samaria. However, they apparently believed that Jesus was exclusive Jewish property. "Now those who had been scattered by the persecution in connection with Stephen traveled as far as Phoenicia, Cyprus and Antioch, telling the message only to Jews."[1] Opinion was divided on this matter, however, as the next verse reports that some went to Antioch and began to speak to Greeks also. God prospered that effort too, as "a great number of people believed and turned to the Lord."

The gospel fit well into existing Jewish religious practices. The Jewish believers retained the synagogue format. They held to the familiar except that now, in Jesus, they had their Messiah! They were now "completed Jews." Everything had finally come together for them. It is understandable that that was the perspective of Jewish believers, so one can understand why the gospel's expansion into the Gentile world created tensions and conflict.

One of the first insights we get into the chasm between the Jewish believers' world and the Gentiles' is the account of the Apostle Peter's visit to Cornelius. Cornelius is described as being "devout and God-fearing; he gave generously to those in need and prayed to God regularly."[2] He was directed by God, in a vision, to send for Peter. Still God had to put Peter through a special preparation even to get him to visit the man. Peter was on a rooftop in Joppa when he, too, had a vision. Three times a sheet filled with nonkosher edibles was lowered to him. Three times Peter refused. Before he could sort it all out, three men sent by Cornelius were at the door. So he went with them. When he got inside Cornelius's house and heard his story, a totally new insight hit Peter. He said, "I now realize how true it is that God . . . accepts men from every nation who fear him."[3] So Peter explained the gospel to Cornelius, and even before he had finished, the Holy Spirit came on the whole household. The Jewish believers with Peter "were astonished that the gift of the Holy Spirit had been poured out even on the Gentiles."[4]

Now, here was a dilemma. Peter had no recourse but to baptize that household, but what would the folks back in Jerusalem say about that? He had already broken the tradition of the elders just by entering Cornelius's house. So, when Peter got back to Jerusalem, the Jewish believers "criticized him and said, 'You went into the house of uncircumcised men and ate with them.'"[5] After Peter explained everything, his critics themselves concluded, "So then, God has even granted the Gentiles repentance unto life."

But the real tensions hadn't even begun.

"THEN FOR THE GENTILE"

We can only speculate why God did not assign one of the original twelve to take the gospel to the Gentiles. He instead employed someone from outside the circle of those who were the fruit of Jesus' earthly ministry. We saw in chapter 4 how well suited the Apostle Paul was for the mission. His religious, cultural, social, and political background was different from that of the Twelve. They were almost all Galileans—unlearned tradesmen. Paul was educated and cosmopolitan. He was a Roman citizen who could pass for an Egyptian in his appearance. Whether these differences had anything to do with God's choice or not, we don't know. All we do know for sure is what God said about the matter: "This man is my chosen instrument to carry my name before the Gentiles and their kings."[6] Paul was, indeed, extraordinary. Never once did he display the sort of ethnocentrism that we saw Peter struggle with—and that most of us struggle with.

The year was AD 46 or 47 when Paul and Barnabas set out on their first missionary journey. It took them into the towns of Galatia, and lasted about eighteen months. They preached the gospel as God had revealed it to Paul: that there is no difference between Jew and Gentile, that justification is by faith in Christ apart from the law.

Apparently, some important people, probably from Jerusalem, did not agree at all. They retraced Paul and Barnabas's route on a missionary journey of their own. Their purpose was to correct Paul's gospel because he had left out the need for circumcision, had not instructed the Gentiles to observe Jewish customs, nor had he told them to keep the special days and feasts.

When Paul heard about this he was angry. He fired off a sharp letter to be circulated among his spiritual offspring in Galatia, refuting the teachings of the countermissionaries. In the letter, he chides, "I am astonished that you are so quickly deserting the one who called you . . . and are turning to a different gospel—which is really no gospel at all. Evidently some people are throwing you into confusion. . . . If anybody is preaching to you a gospel other than what you accepted, let him be eternally condemned!"[7] He implicates Peter as an accessory to the confusion: "When Peter came to Antioch, I opposed him to his face, because he was clearly in the wrong. . . . He was afraid of those who belonged to the circumcision group."[8] Paul called Peter a hypocrite and even criticized his own partner, Barnabas, for giving in under the pressure.

Paul threw down the gauntlet. He was ready to go to war. What, we ask, was the issue? The countermissionaries were not questioning the essentials. They believed in the deity of Jesus Christ, His death, and His resurrection as fervently as Paul did. They accepted the authority of the Scriptures. They believed in justification by faith. Their only concerns were matters of Jewish customs, like what and with whom one eats; the days, months, seasons, and years to be observed; and the necessity of circumcision.[9]

For Paul, those extras were tantamount to a total destruction of the gospel. He said, "Mark my words! I, Paul, tell you that if you let yourselves be circumcised, Christ will be of no value to you at all."[10] That was a strange statement. All Jewish believers were circumcised, and they continued to practice circumcision. Was Christ, then, of no value to them either? Not at all! Inconsistent? Not at all. We will see why as we go along.

THE WATERSHED EVENT FOR THE FUTURE OF THE GOSPEL

The whole matter soon wound up in court. Leaders from both the local and the traveling expressions of God's people convened in Jerusalem. I am unsure of the sequence of the events—whether the letter to the Galatians was written first, or whether the Jerusalem debate came first. I guess it really doesn't matter, as there was no confusion regarding the issues.

One side maintained that "unless you are circumcised according to the custom taught by Moses, you cannot be saved."[11] The other said, no, "A man is not justified by observing the law, but by faith in Jesus Christ."[12]

Paul and Barnabas did not have an open-and-shut case. The opposition had a lot of sympathy, support, and the teaching of Moses to back them up: "They must be circumcised. My covenant in your flesh is to be an everlasting covenant."[13] How would anybody get out from under that statement?

It is important to notice what constituted evidence in this debate. Somewhere in the middle of the discussion, Peter told his Cornelius story, and it is apparent that he had learned his lesson from the experience. He said, "God . . . showed that he accepted them by giving the Holy Spirit to them, just as he did to us. . . . He purified their hearts by faith."[14] Then Peter brilliantly puts his finger on the core issue: "Why do you try to test God by putting on the necks of the disciples a yoke that neither we nor our fathers have been able to bear?"[15] The next testimony on the agenda came from Barnabas and Paul. They told of the miraculous things God had done among the Gentiles through them. They told war stories. God's blessing on their efforts demonstrated His approval.

Finally, James spoke up and said, yes, and what they are doing fits with Scripture. He quoted from Amos. His conclusion, echoing Peter's observation, was, "We should not make it difficult for the Gentiles who are turning to God."[16] Every Christian should write that statement down and magnetize it to the refrigerator door.

The defense was based on three things: Peter's experience with Cornelius, which demonstrated that God could work outside the precincts of Jewish structures and traditions; the obvious blessing of God on Paul's efforts; and the Bible. On the basis of those arguments, the gospel of Christ was declared distinct from Jewish tradition.

What Was at Stake?

What if that decision had gone the other way? If Paul and Barnabas had lost this debate, they would have had to go back to Galatia and say, "Sorry, folks, we were wrong. We are going to have to circumcise everybody. And our next study will be in Leviticus, to make sure you've got the feasts and customs down pat. From there we'll go on to the Mishnah."

The purity and the mobility of the gospel was hanging in the balance that day. How far would the Christian movement have gotten had Paul and Barnabas lost this debate? They won the freedom to offer a clean gospel to the Gentile world—a gospel that was free of cultural and traditional trappings.

To require people to embrace anything beyond what is written in Scripture is to put a yoke on their necks that they will not be able to bear. Anything more than Scripture is too much. This has been a constant, recurring tension throughout history. It is a tension today. We can't seem to resist including a few amendments to the gospel of grace.

Paradox!

The manner in which this first major conflict was handled offers us a treasury of practical guidance in how to preserve unity in the midst of diversity. Unity is not uniformity or conformity. *Unity depends upon the ability to affirm and actively support diversity.* There must be room for diversity in the way the body finds its expression, because the world to which we are sent is diverse.

What did not happen in the wake of the Jerusalem debate is as significant as what did happen. Paul and Barnabas had won. It was agreed that circumcision and the observance of Jewish law were unnecessary for salvation.

The believers in Antioch, Syria, and Cilicia were anxiously awaiting the outcome. So the leaders composed a letter containing the decision and sent it back to Antioch via Paul, Barnabas, Silas, and Judas. Then Paul and Silas set out to carry the good news to the believers in Syria and Cilicia. On the way Paul picked up a new team member, Timothy—and the first thing he did was to circumcise him!

Now what was that all about? Hadn't Paul and Barnabas just come away from a debate in which it was decided that circumcision was unnecessary? Hadn't Paul penned the words, "If you let yourselves be circumcised, Christ will be of no value to you at all"?[17] Why on earth, then, did Paul circumcise Timothy? The explanation given in the text is, "He circumcised him because of the Jews who lived in that area."[18] But that still doesn't seem to make much sense. Imagine the confusion in the minds of the believers Paul visited with the news that circumcision was unnecessary, with Timothy right there limping along beside him.

An event recorded in Acts 21 adds to the puzzle, and to its clarification. Here Paul makes his final visit to Jerusalem. His hosts' response was mixed, as by then Paul was a highly controversial figure. The leaders, James and the elders, were glad to see him. They spent the first day, or days, telling each other stories. Paul "reported in detail what God had done among the Gentiles through his ministry." Then it was time for the people from Jerusalem to tell their story. They said to Paul, "You see, brother, how many thousands of Jews have believed, and all of them are zealous for the law."[19]

What? What was the Acts 15 debate all about? Hadn't they decided that lawkeeping was unnecessary? But here the Jerusalem elders are concerned about the simple fact that Paul had shown up in town! They said, these thousands of Jews who have come to believe have heard about you. They hear "that you teach all the Jews who live among the Gentiles to turn away from Moses, telling them not to circumcise their children or live according to our customs. What shall we do? They will certainly hear that you have come."[20] His presence was a threat to unity.

I think there was truth to that report about Paul. He did teach the Jews involved in his ministry among the Gentiles to adapt to those they were bringing to Christ.[21] But here in Jerusalem, Paul, for the sake of preserving unity, agreed to shave his head and go through Jewish rites of purification. He was practicing what he preached—"To the Jews I became like a Jew, to win the Jews. . . . To those not having the law I became like one not having the law."[22]

Perhaps finally we can make some sense of all this. From the Acts 15 debate on, the people of God took on two distinct expressions: a Jewish expression, and a Gentile expression. Galatians 2 makes it clear that this was, indeed, the case.

Two Variations of God's People

In Galatians 2, Paul describes a critical meeting of a half-dozen key leaders—James, Peter, John, Barnabas, Titus, and himself—held in Jerusalem. The subject was what to do about the growing tension between Jewish and Gentile believers that was beginning to threaten the ability of the Gentiles to understand the gospel.

Paul was highly motivated to convene that meeting. Paul talks about this private meeting as follows: "I set before them the gospel that I preach among the Gentiles . . . for fear that I was running or had run my race in vain."[23] Paul was concerned that everything he had done would be wiped out. If those countermissionaries operating out of Jerusalem kept at it, kept visiting and confusing the Gentile believers, they would destroy the gospel for the Gentiles.

Peter, James, and John agreed with Paul's preaching. Then the six of them came up with a very helpful insight, which in turn resolved the whole problem! Paul reports: "They saw that I had been entrusted with the task of preaching the gospel to the Gentiles, just as Peter had been to the Jews."[24] They decided the work among the Jews and the work among the Gentiles were of such different natures that it would be best to treat the two movements separately. Paul continues, "They agreed that we should go to the Gentiles, and they to the Jews."[25] This decision did not disunite the people of God, it simply allowed for needed diversity and made provision for it. The decision to diversify preserved the unity of the body. There was a Jewish expression of the body, and there was a Gentile expression. The differences were culturally designed.

LESSONS FROM THE FIRST CENTURY

The experience of these first-generation believers is a rich source of guidance for us as we face the challenge of getting to that large part of our own society that is unlike ourselves. In chapters 1 and 2 we saw how people as close as next door can be worlds apart from us in the way they think—and headed in the opposite direction. It may be inconceivable to us that the sanctuaries, hymns, and sermons that we take for granted, and that we find so meaningful, do nothing for such people—that is, if we even manage to bring them with us at all. Are we ready to admit that if such people are ever to know Christ and become a part of His people, it will have to happen on their turf? Our approach to them must be according to their needs, in ways that are meaningful to them. Would we be comfortable encouraging that kind of diversity?

Two lessons stand out from the first-century example that help clarify what might be entailed in taking the gospel to the unreached American.

Cultural Differences Are Real

The first major crisis for God's people was a culture clash—but the Jews thought the issues were doctrinal. They couldn't imagine life without Moses and the Law. The special days, months, and years were their Christmas, New Year, and Fourth of July. Over the centuries the laws of Moses had become more than religion, they had become deeply ingrained traditions that gave them their identity as a people.

But the Gentiles couldn't live with those traditions. Because they were unfamiliar, the Gentiles would have gotten confused over what was grace and what was Jewish. And in the confusion, that slippery truth of justification by faith would have gotten lost. Thus Paul was adamant about protecting the Gentiles from Jewish influence. The Jews could simultaneously maintain their traditions and "grace by faith," whereas the Gentiles would have thought that keeping all those unfamiliar laws was what made their relationship with God possible. That's human nature.

Paul illustrates this by telling a story about Simon Peter's visit to Antioch, during which he ate with the Gentiles. After all, he had been liberated by the Cornelius experience! But then some of James' men showed up from Jerusalem. Peter, knowing what those men believed about Jews and Gentiles eating together and not wanting to take the heat, went over and sat with the Jews.

When James' people entered the room, they found everything in order. But the Apostle Paul was watching, and like any good spiritual parent, he knew that his primary responsibility lay with his spiritual children. And Paul could imagine what was going on in their minds. As Peter left their company to join the Jewish believers who were arriving, Paul realized those Gentile believers could draw only one conclusion—that they were second-class citizens. To be truly accepted, they had to be thinking, they would need to begin to observe the special days, the customs, and circumcision in the same way the Jewish believers did.

Paul, realizing those Gentile believers could never do that without losing their understanding of grace by faith in the confusion, confronted Peter before everyone. He told Peter his behavior was hypocritical and that he was forcing the Gentiles to follow Jewish customs.

When new Christians are required to take on a new set of customs in order to become insiders, they are in danger of getting their understanding of grace by faith mixed up. They will also become outsiders to their own people. This is so obvious, but so often we ignore it.

While writing this chapter I received a letter from a young missionary in Brazil who had gotten to know some of my Brazilian brothers. He observed their faith and their outreach, commenting, "I feel that the group is doing an excellent job of local evangelism, probably the best job I have ever seen. Most individuals are involved and it is not an easy-believism approach."

But it bothers this missionary that these Christians are "not organized," and in the letter he describes his desire to institute "a structure and organization that makes people accountable for doctrine and moral behavior." He wants corporate worship, organized giving, and so on.

What this missionary does not realize is that most of the things he wants to institute are already there, and have been for years. Nothing disorganized will self-perpetuate for twenty-five years, expanding in many cities across a country as has this expression of God's people. The organization is invisible to this young missionary because it is not in the form he is accustomed to seeing. His paradigm is different. In my response to him, I said that what he was seeing *is* already organized, and that if he were to attempt to implement his ideas, they would produce the same effect they have produced in the United States, where Christians are frequently passive and where few actively and fruitfully share their faith.

This is the problem I see all over the world in so many church-planting efforts. The church planter starts with a blueprint in mind, knowing what a church looks like because he or she was raised in one. But God's people are to expand not by producing replicas of a structure, but by bringing unbelievers to faith and then meeting their needs. As the new believers proceed through life together, the appropriate forms are agreed upon and emerge to facilitate biblical functions. Every flock should have its own characteristics. I believe that is why Jesus commanded us to go, make disciples, and teach them to obey all His commands. If we restrict ourselves to helping people follow Christ and refrain from insisting on the forms that following will take, forms will emerge that fit the people and their needs.

As each flock finds its own expression within the context of biblical truth, there will be diversity. It is important that this diversity exist for two reasons. First, the forms of corporate living must fit the needs and the culture of those being reached. Second, the forms should not seem alien or unnecessarily odd to the unbelievers who are observing. It is our absorption with tidiness that leads us to attempt to bring all cultures and classes of people under the same roof. But the fact that we cannot do that does not imply disunity. It is simply the acknowledgment of the reality of cultural diversity.

Freedom Is the Prerequisite
to Serving People According to Their Needs

The book of Galatians has been the basic text for this chapter. *Prisoner*, *locked up*, *slavery*, and *supervision* are recurring words in this book. Its theme could be called, "Freedom and Slavery."

Who is the slave master? Sin, we say. That's right. That's what Jesus said—"Anyone who sins is a slave to sin." In Paul's letter to the Galatians he says, "The Scripture declares that the whole world is a prisoner of sin,"[26] and that the jail keeper is the law!

That seems clear enough.We sin, and then do it again. It becomes a habit, then a way of life. We think little of that sin because everyone else is doing the same thing. Then we come across God's law. It frightens us because we suddenly realize what we're doing is wrong, and we will be judged by God for that wrong. So we decide to quit sinning, and we find we cannot! It's at that point that we realize we are in a prison cell of our own making. We try the door and it's locked! We are trapped.

Paul indicates another previously unidentified jail keeper. He says, "We were in slavery under *the basic principles of the world.*"[27] The word he uses is *stoicheia*. The word refers to the deification of the elements, the worship of air and matter—the basic materials of which everything in the cosmos, including man, is composed. In short he's talking about the pagan religion out of which the Galatians had come to embrace Christ. Pagan religions enslave. The powers of the sun, wind, and star gods were threatening, terrible powers that leave people trapped in fearful superstition. Paul reminds them that God sent His Son to redeem from all that. They are no longer slaves. They are sons! They are free.

Then Paul asks why, now that they are free and know God, would they consider going back to *stoicheia*? "Why on earth would you ever want to get back into such slavery?"

The Galatians weren't considering dusting off their old gods— Zeus, Ares, and the lot. They were enslaving themselves by getting involved in the Jewish traditions, observing Jewish feast and fast days, switching to kosher food and getting circumcised. Certainly mixing a little Judaism with one's faith in Christ isn't as bad as praying to the stars! After all, both Christ and the Law come from the same book. But according to Paul, either the pagan or Jewish system—*any* system of human origin—is *stoicheia*. A little Jewish traditon superimposed on Christ will enslave you just as quickly as Zeus will.

Systems. Human beings seem to have a perverse, irresistible need to turn whatever they believe into a system that they promptly use to enslave themselves and everyone around them. We do this repeatedly with the Christian faith, endangering the easily obscured truth of grace every time. We say, "If you want to be a good Christian, here are a few things you must give up. And here are some things you must be sure to do. And don't forget to show up at the following times. If you do these things you will please God and us." When we do that, matters that really count and are able to produce true spiritual transformation are lost.

In the book of Colossians, the Apostle Paul also uses *stoicheia* in a similar way. Here he says, "Since you died with Christ to the basic principles [*stoicheia*] of this world, why, as though you still belonged to it, do you submit to its rules: 'Do not handle! Do not taste! Do not touch!'? These are all destined to perish . . . because they are based on human commands and teachings. Such regulations indeed have an appearance of wisdom . . . but they lack any value in restraining sensual indulgence."[28]

As we shall see in the next chapter, the entire religious system of the Pharisees was based on the premise that goodness—righteousness—is a matter of getting the system spelled out and then keeping it. My colleague Aldo Berndt observes that Jesus put His finger on the futility of pursuing righteousness through the observance of such a system of regulations. Jesus said, "If your right eye causes you to sin, gouge it out and throw it away." "Even if someone would go so far as to practice such a rule," observed Aldo, "that person would see impurity through the bleeding hole in his head." Rule-keeping doesn't solve the problems of our flesh. Yet we all tend to construct our systems for behavior, it being far easier to follow a system than to honestly confront the real issues. But such systems don't bring true transformation. That must come from within, by the hand of the Spirit of God.

So, we conclude that whatever the system or whatever the religion, there is no freedom outside of Christ. And Paul is fearful that believers who entrap themselves in some system will lose their freedom. Thus he writes, "It is for freedom that Christ has set us free. Stand firm, then, and do not let yourselves be burdened again by a yoke of slavery."[29]

We are free, free from the enslavement of sin and human systems of religion and tradition! But what to do with that freedom? The whole world longs for freedom. Our Declaration of Independence is a statement that we Americans choose death over subjugation. Countless people under Communist rule abandoned their families and all their possessions and fled to the West to gain freedom. I often wonder what people do with the freedom they pay so dearly to gain. How does it really improve the quality of everyday life for them? Or are they like the dog chasing the car? If he did catch it, he would have no idea as to what to do with it.

But our freedom, hard-won by Christ, is necessary to God's purpose for us. Paul explains what we are to do with our freedom: "You, my brothers, were called to be free. But do not use your freedom to indulge the sinful nature; rather, [use it to] serve one another in love."[30] Freedom means not being bound to a human system or agenda. As such, freedom allows us to serve others according to *their* needs. I do not have to bring a person into my system, or into my particular fellowship, in order to help him or her. We can operate on that person's agenda, according to his or her needs. This is what it really means to be "receiver-oriented."

CONCLUSION

As we minister to both the believer and the unbeliever, we can summarize all of this in one question: Who adjusts to whom? Do those who minister adjust to those to whom they minister, or is it the other way around? As the Apostle Paul made new plantings of the gospel where Christ was not known, he was careful to be "all things to all men so that by all possible means I might save some."[31]

Freedom in adaptation has two applications. The first is in relationship to the unbeliever. Here we need to be willing to set aside our forms of religious practices, our scruples of conduct in questionable matters, our elaborate doctrines that will only serve to confound the simplicity of the gospel to the searching unbeliever, and even our religious vocabulary. We need to go where unbelievers are and build relationships with them within the context of their world. We need to adapt to them and feel comfortable in their presence and in their circumstances. We need to love them and accept them without regard to the prospect of leading them to a knowledge of Christ. This is genuine adaptation.

The second application to freedom is in relationships among the people of God. In the first century the people of God accommodated

major disagreements because of the value they placed on understanding grace through faith in Christ by both Jew and Gentile.
We who make up the church in this country need the same
breadth of vision. Frequently today diversity is cause for sus-
picion rather than celebration. Accusations of illegitimacy are
raised between various parts of the body. We use our suspicions to
justify our competitiveness. These attitudes debilitate the church.
Our lack of unity stands as a barrier to effective communication to
the unbelieving world to whom we are sent. To move from where
we are to the kind of freedom and diversity in unity that we have
just seen among God's people in the first century is extremely
difficult.

This acceptance of diversity needs to permeate all manifes-
tations of God's people, including both the local and the apostolic, or mobile, functions. None of us owns the franchise on the
gospel!

CHAPTER EIGHT

To Freedom and Diversity

▼

Human nature and tradition consort together to defeat us in our quest for freedom and diversity.

We have seen how God's people in the first century struggled to free themselves from the cocoon of Jewish tradition to make the message of the gospel accessible to the whole world. It was a healthy struggle, one that taught them that diversity is an essential virtue, not a weakness. It takes all kinds to reach all kinds. Diversity allows God's people to cut a broader swath through the world with the gospel.

That diversity is a virtue should come as no surprise. God apparently loves it! Look at nature. In His infinite creativity, no two of any species He has ever made are exactly alike. His creation is extravagant in its diversity. Wherever we may look, whether in the mountains, on the plains, in the forests, or under the sea, we are struck by the profusion of the variety in His work. God apparently enjoys this diversity He has made. He describes, with satisfaction, the characteristics of the behemoth:

> "Look at the behemoth,
>> which I made along with you
>> and which feeds on grass like an ox.

What strength he has in his loins,
>   what power in the muscles of his belly! . . .
The hills bring him their produce,
>   and all the wild animals play nearby."[1]

Then, concerning the crocodile, He asks,

"Can you pull in the leviathan with a fishhook
>   or tie down his tongue with a rope? . . .
Can you make a pet of him like a bird
>   or put him on a leash for your girls? . . .
Nothing on earth is his equal—
>   a creature without fear.
He looks down on all that are haughty;
>   he is king over all that are proud."[2]

These are words that master artists might use in explaining to the viewer the thoughts that inspired their masterpieces.

Diversity will characterize the multitude who will worship the Lamb—people from "every tribe and language and people and nation"[3] will be there. It would surprise me if He does not preserve this diversity throughout eternity, even as He transforms us all into the image of His Son.

INCORRIGIBLY ETHNOCENTRIC

Why, then, do most of us struggle with diversity? Why are we so much more comfortable with conformity? Perhaps it is because the human being is by nature, perhaps by necessity, ethnocentric. We previously defined ethnocentrism as the belief in the inherent superiority of one's own group and culture. It is that tendency we all have of using our own ways of doing things as the measuring stick. We laugh at the way people in the next state talk; and the folks on the coast, why, you would hardly call that English! Funny how you and I are the only ones who really speak without an accent. Every culture is ethnocentric. Almost all of us think our ways are the best and that others are inferior.

Some ethnocentrism is necessary for survival. We must love

and be loyal to our families if they are to survive. A father must prefer his child to other children. The same holds true for a nation. Its citizens must be content that their way of life is worthy to be preserved if it is to continue. They must believe that certain things are worth fighting for—dying for, if necessary.

Ethnocentrism begets tradition. Tradition is the handing down of beliefs and customs from one generation to another. All of us live under the influence of these two forces. Life would be unimaginable without them. We all need a place and opinions by which to orient ourselves. We need to have an inside, a people, a way of life. Many of our daily habits have their origin in our traditions. It starts out first thing in the morning. Our traditions help us decide what to wear, what to eat for breakfast, and when to eat it. They tell us how to greet people we meet, according to the level of intimacy. Strangers receive a certain greeting, while another is reserved for intimate friends. Traditions instruct us on our behavior when we enter a home. Do we remove our shoes, or leave them on? Do we kiss the hostess, or ignore her entirely? They tell us when to leave and how to do it. Do we just get up and walk out, or do we first make the rounds to give a personal farewell to everyone in the house?

Traditions coach us through a thousand decisions a day, and we seldom, if ever, stop to think about it. They make life comfortably predictable. They make us insiders and give us a sense of place.

Personal identity is also related to the traditions of a culture. Every culture has its own tradition in art, music, dress, cuisine, etc. As we grow up we acquire favorites in each of these areas within the range of choices approved by the culture. One person prefers rock over pop; another jazz over classics. We take a certain pride in our choices, whatever they might be. Through our choices we affirm both our belonging and our individuality.

National pride depends upon tradition for its nourishment. Red, white, and blue arranged into stars and stripes; the national anthem; tales of the nation's heroes, of the framing of the Constitution—such have the power to elicit powerful emotions. Individual identity is tied to national identity.

It is no wonder that it feels so good to get back home after spending a period of time in a foreign country. To be in a place where those countless, subconscious daily decisions are suddenly forced into the conscious level can be a lot of work. When in a foreign country we wear ourselves out trying to pick up on how to handle even mundane matters. A couple of suppressed giggles and a stare or two painfully remind us that we stick out, even as we struggle to discover what proper behavior might be for that moment. Under the stress of the situation the temptation can become irresistible to make unfavorable comparisons between our host country and our own. With time, "picturesque" is redefined as "strange," and "strange" soon comes to mean "backward, irrational, inefficient," and worse. When we get to that stage, we are wearing our ethnocentrism on our sleeve for all to see.

So we live with the dilemma. We are ethnocentric by nature. We therefore need a certain narrowness, a certain degree of conformity for the sake of our own mental health, as individuals and as a people. How then can we also be true advocates of diversity?

FREEDOM, THE COUNTERBALANCE

It is here that the freedom we have in Christ becomes all important. An understanding of this freedom serves to counterbalance our ethnocentrism. Jesus tells us, "So if the Son sets you free, you will be free indeed."[4] And Paul tells us, too: "It is for freedom that Christ has set us free."[5] For what purpose? To "serve one another in love."[6]

Christ has set us free. In this passage Paul is telling the Galatian Christians that they are free from a particular set of traditions. God has given them a new place, a new identity. So it is with us. We have a higher citizenship. We are citizens of God's Kingdom and members of His household. This does not mean we no longer give value to the traditions of our society. Rather, it means we are freed from their control. Their mastery over us is broken because we have already taken our place alongside Christ in the "heavenly realm." There is another "place" where we belong. Theoretically, we who have Christ should be among those who enjoy the good things of our culture the most. We have a perspective that allows us the freedom to appreciate what is good and leave the rest, freed from the control of ethnocentrism and its traditions. Not only are we freed from their control, we are freed from the compulsion to impose them on others.

This perspective enables us to be true servants. What's the tie between freedom and service? We have observed that we are all ethnocentric, as is the person we are serving. He or she finds a sense of place, of identity, in his or her own set of traditions, just as we do in ours. This may not be a big issue where the one who serves and the one being served share a common ethos. But that is the exception. Most people, certainly those not raised in our church environments, are substantially different from us. This faces us with a critical question when we meet with such people: Who is to win? Who gets to hold on to their ways, and who gives in?

Our standard procedure is to call on the one being served to adapt to the one who serves. He or she is the newcomer to our fellowship, or perhaps new in Christ. Since we are comfortable in our ways and find them meaningful to us, we assume others will find the same comfort and meaning once they get into the swing of doing things our way. And besides, we reason, our ways are "more Christian." Changes are rightfully in order for the other person. We want that person to conform to biblical mandates of morality, but we also impose our scruples. Scruples are the traditional behavior patterns of a group, which are given religious justification.

More often than not, when the person being served conforms to traditions and scruples, there is a serious loss. Both sides lose. Where unnecessary changes are imposed, it is easy for the new believer to confuse the cultural changes we expect of him or her with the spiritual changes God intends. Often when there is confusion on this point, the person does what is humanly expected and stops there. He or she stops short of the grace of God and substitutes conformity for real spiritual growth. Understanding grace is foundational to all spiritual growth: "All over the world this gospel is bearing fruit and growing, just as it has been doing among you *since the day you heard it and understood God's grace in all its truth.*"[7]

In addition, those surface identity changes often cost the new believer his or her rapport with family and peers. Thus the possibility for the gospel to expand naturally among that person's network has been destroyed. We should avoid calling upon new believers to behave in ways that make them unnecessarily strange in the eyes of their nonbelieving peers.

Freedom is the guardian of diversity. Our innate ethnocentrism craves conformity. We tend to confuse unity with conformity. Insistence on conformity is a social blending machine that would beat us all into a single, bland flavor. But freedom says, "Leave them be." God makes no distinction between us and them: "Their hearts, just like ours, have been purified by faith."[8] If we are to go as God's people to this society gone pagan, we are going to need a firm grasp on this matter. We need to know how to help people conform to God's Son according to God's Word within the context of their own ethos.

TRADITION AND TRADITIONALISM

Jaroslav Pelikan, in his work *Vindication of Tradition*, makes an important distinction. "Tradition," he says, "is the living faith of the dead, [whereas] traditionalism is the dead faith of the living."[9]

Traditions are established customs, often handed down through the generations and generally observed. Traditionalism is the excessive respect for tradition that gives it the status of divine revelation.

Our contemporary church walks the razor's edge between tradition and traditionalism. Although we may affirm our commitment to the Scriptures as our sole authority, things are not that simple in practice. Most of us regularly lose our balance and fall into traditionalism. We get stuck in the past.

Several years ago I was invited to spend a week with a group of missionaries of a certain organization in Brazil. When they invited me, they explained that they were having little difficulty leading people to Christ. Their problem was that they were unable to draw their converts into their churches. They wanted me to teach on this subject.

The thrust of my teaching was similar to what I have been

saying in this book. My suggestion was, when you win people, don't even try to dislocate them. Rather, continue to evangelize until you have led others of the same family and barrio to Christ. In that way a nucleus will form and your new believers will wake up one morning to find themselves "churched." It will have surrounded them.

After several days of working through the Scriptures on these ideas, the field leader spoke up and said, "Your organization obviously gives you the freedom to go to the Scriptures, go out and experiment, and then go back to the Scriptures, and keep doing that until you think you've gotten it right. I suggest we all resign and join up with you."

I was embarrassed. Was that what I was communicating, that my mission was better than theirs? I quickly attempted to patch things up. I said, "I'm not suggesting that you reject your past. Give thanks for what God has done through you. Preserve it with care. Only when you go to the next city, or barrio, do things differently. Try applying the things we've been talking about here."

At that, another missionary replied, "You don't understand our situation. We don't have the freedom to just go to the Bible and then go out and apply it like you do."

That is traditionalism. Although those missionaries probably would have defended the authority of Scripture with their lives, they did not have the liberty to use it freely. Their past was in control of their future. This kind of thing goes on all the time in our missionary efforts around the world.

I have a friend who lives and ministers in one of the most secular societies in the world. After several years of barrenness he decided to take a radical step—to stop talking and just listen for an entire year. He spent the following year hanging out wherever people naturally congregated. There he would just listen and ask questions. He refrained from talking about Christ. He emerged from the year with a new understanding of the people, their values and needs. Then he went to the Scriptures and prepared himself to address those values and needs with biblical truth. Very creative! The fruit was not long in coming.

When I visited this friend a few months later, I found him surrounded by about fifty young believers. In that country, that kind of response constituted a significant breakthrough.

But to my dismay, I discovered that those fifty young people were busily engaged in reproducing the forms of their all but defunct state church in their new fellowship. They had formalized certain offices and activities, and they were making good progress on their hymnal. They had even sent the brightest of the lot off to seminary to prepare to be their pastor.

As a result of all this, what could have been the beginning of a movement of the gospel in that desperately needy country turned out to be a cul-de-sac. Their unbelieving peers, at first attracted and intrigued by the faith of those new Christians, concluded that what they were witnessing was nothing more than a return to something they had already judged to be hopelessly irrelevant: their state church. They turned away.

By the time these young believers realized what was happening, it was already too late. Church forms are like cement. Once they are in place, they are there for the duration. That group never did grow beyond the original fifty. I found myself wondering what prompts even the most creative among us to do things like that, to suddenly revert to traditionalism as these people did.

TRADITIONALISM AND THE CHURCH IN AMERICA

If the missionary effort can be so easily controlled by the forms of the past, the church in America runs an even greater risk. We have several hundred years of unbroken history in which our churches have evolved into their present forms. In spite of our many denominations and subdenominations, and in spite of our doctrinal differences, the commonalities still far outnumber the differences. We are pretty much in consensus on church forms and practices. Seldom do we give serious thought or discussion to the influences the growing cultural differences in America might have on the forms and practices of our churches.

Remember our thesis: God's people are in the world to bear witness to the world, and the ministry, both within and without, depends upon every believer. But if we would evaluate our practices against our thesis, we would have to admit to some major omissions and misdirections in the essential functions of our contemporary churches.

These are not secondary matters. We are talking about the essentials of God's plan for making the news of His Son known to the world. We often find that our traditions are in conflict with these essentials. I believe that we are faced with either significant change in our present institutions, or new beginnings outside of them.

I have a friend who was a part of a team that set out to start a church that would be committed to the principles we are talking about here. The team gave priority to the training of elders. The congregation was divided into house churches, each of which was assigned an elder who helped shepherd the members of that house church. Centralized activities were kept at a minimum for the sake of keeping people free to minister to their families and unbelieving friends.

The weekly gatherings were dynamic. I will never forget the first one I visited. People of all sorts were there, from men in business suits to ponytails. Many were new believers. The Bible teaching was down to earth, aimed at people's needs. I loved it.

So did most everyone else who visited. The word got around and soon the migratory flock from neighboring churches came pouring in. Their needs consumed the energies of the leaders of this young church. Their wants gradually set the agenda. The inertia of the traditions of these migrants engulfed this very creative effort and shaped it accordingly. This church continues to be an outstanding body of people. It continues to enjoy godly, gifted leadership, and it continues to be a very powerful ministry.

So what's the problem, we ask? The problem is that the vision that original team had for taking the church into society through the efforts of every believer was frustrated. The pastors have told me that the needs for care among those who come are so consuming that there is no energy left to get out beyond their own front door. This is a very common problem in our churches. An attractive church will grow, but those who come, in the main, do not come out of the world but from the neighboring churches. And they come with clear ideas of what they want in a church. Eventually those ideas prevail. Thus there is an inertia in the church in this country that overcomes the bright new ideas, devours and eventually buries them. The struggle is with traditionalism.

Congregating as a Tradition

We hold strong convictions on the importance of the gathering of the church. "Forsake not the assembling of yourselves together" is our refrain. We are good at congregating. Where we have trouble is with some of the other equally essential functions of the church.

God's people are not, in essence, a congregation. They are community. "Congregation" is frequently used in the Old Testament to describe the gathering of the people of Israel. "Community" implies life together, a life of caring for one another that touches the full spectrum of our affairs.

We recognize the importance of our gathering for teaching and worship, but congregating has the absolute priority as the predominant form in our churches. We are less clear that we are to live as a community in full view of and among unbelievers. If these were in balance today, the forms of our church would be different beyond recognition. So we proceed, mildly concerned that we "aren't doing more in the area of outreach." Generally, when it comes to outreach, the average believer is left to make his or her own way. It is just not a part of our tradition to plan for our being in the world with the same serious commitment, with the same disposition to invest people, time, and money, as it is for us to provide for our congregating.

This imbalance of commitment often puts Christians who feel called to put their gifts and efforts to use among unbelievers into tension with the rest of the body, if not with their own conscience.

Tensions

One of my personal priorities, as our family moved out of Brazil into a new neighborhood in the states, was to find some friends among our neighbors. The first opportunity presented itself, literally, within the first few minutes after we pulled up in front of our new house.

A neighbor family came out to greet us and to see if they could be of help. Dave and I quickly discovered that we were both joggers. As we compared our schedules to find a common free time, Dave said, "There is one time during the week when I'm always free. That's on Sunday mornings."

My mind raced as I had to decide on the spot. My witness with him was on the line. So I said, "Fine, let's make it 8:00 a.m." Sunday morning found me out jogging the trails around our house with my new neighbor. As we ran we talked. From what I was learning about him, I realized his pilgrimage to Christ needed time. Our program evolved to "reading and running." We would spend an hour or so examining the book of Romans before hitting the trails. This wiped out my Sunday mornings.

Dave was right. Sunday mornings were conflict-free, not only for him, but for everyone else in our neighborhood. After a busy week at work and a Saturday filled with chores such as fixing faucets, taking the dog to get a shot, and doing the supermarket, Sunday morning was the time to kick back and relax. It was time to walk, to smell the roses, to chat with a neighbor. Sundays soon found me involved with the people around us from sunup to sundown.

My life is further complicated by the fact that my work keeps me traveling about half the time. This makes it difficult to be consistent with anything I attempt to do in my hometown. I soon found myself struggling to balance my already divided time between my involvement with my neighbors and my involvement with our church. Sundays were the focal point of my tensions. There was no way for me to feel good about Sundays.

As I would sit in church, I would find myself visualizing our neighborhood, imagining all those people out there, some of whom were dropping broad hints that they too would like to look at the Bible with us—if I would ever find the time for them! I would sit there feeling guilty. So the next Sunday would be given to my neighbors. As I would spend the day with them, I would find myself wondering what I was missing at the church. I'd miss the people, the sermon. Something had to give. I invited my pastor to have lunch with me to discuss the matter.

Over lunch I explained my dilemma. The crux of the matter is that unbelieving neighbors owe us nothing. If we want to go to them, it has to be on their terms, at their convenience, and on their turf. Although they might be interested in hearing what we have for them, they are far from being willing to go to a church to get it, especially on a Sunday morning! So there we were, I explained to my pastor, with eternal destinies at stake and with my conscience going off the chart in both directions!

We ate our lunch and wondered what to do.

Then I suggested that perhaps the problem lies, in part, in our basic assumptions about the church. Does it not seem odd, I wondered to him, that I could be there in my neighborhood, teaching the Bible to some neighbors who had yet to decide whether or not they were going to believe, and consider that as being outside the ministry of the church? What if I transferred my efforts to the church building? Would that make me an insider? Is the church, then, to be defined by geography? Perhaps our problem is that our definitions of "church," our ecclesiology, draws such a small circle that certain functions essential to its existence cannot even be fitted into it. Could we not, I asked my pastor, draw our circle big enough to include what I was doing in my neighborhood? That thought seemed reasonable to both of us.

Then the pastor asked, "What are you going to do when these people come to Christ?" That, I replied, was impossible to predict. Where these people would eventually find their fellowship would depend, in part, on where they would find their "sense of place." It could even turn out that the body for them would take shape right there on our street.

This conversation with my pastor was an important one for me. We are friends, and I want him to understand and approve of what I'm doing. I have solved my problem, to a point, thanks to the unusual capacity of this pastor to understand. But I am still not at peace.

It is one thing for me to successfully arrange for the freedom I need within my own fellowship to exercise the function I believe God wants me to perform. But I know there are hundreds of others in the body in this country who hunger for involvement with their unbelieving friends of the nature I am describing here. But their chances are slim. Who will equip and empower these people? Who will let them go, grant them the freedom, and then give them the leadership they need? What I am talking about is not, and never has been, a part of our modern ecclesiology. Consequently, I find myself wondering if it is even feasible to hope that we as God's people can break out in this manner. The obstacles are in our own minds, and they are formidable. We are trapped in our own traditionalism.

Are we indeed bound, obliged to endlessly repeat worn patterns, all the while lamenting our impotency to do anything about them? The inertia we are dealing with here resides in the interplay between form and function. Both of these words have appeared repeatedly in the previous paragraphs. An understanding of what they mean and how they work can help us with the answers to the issues we are dealing with.

FORM AND FUNCTION

Function: A necessary or natural action. Example: To
    sit down.
Form: The pattern or shape that facilitates the function.
    Example: A chair.

◆ Function: Cooking, eating, sleeping
◆ Form: A house

◆ Function: Transportation
◆ Form: An automobile

◆ Function: Bible teaching
◆ Form: A sermon

It was in an art class at the University of Minnesota that I first heard the terms *form* and *function*. A student presented a special project she had done. It was a single large canvas with human figures scattered across it. Beside each figure was an everyday object—a chair, a bicycle, a telephone, a cup—each obviously drawn according to the contour of the figure. She had titled the canvas "Form and Function." I wondered what it meant. I also wondered why the professor was so fascinated by that piece of work. I was unimpressed. Only later did I come to realize that that student was exploring the most fundamental principle of design: the form of an object should be determined by its function, or use. The architect or artisan who truly understands this principle can transform something mundane, like a chair, into an exquisite and timeless piece of art.

The next time I thought about form and function was several years later. We were just beginning our ministry in Brazil and were engrossed in discovering how to communicate the gospel to a predominantly Marxist student world that had rejected the religious institutions of its society, virtually in mass. Our ministry was driven by the two truths that constitute the thesis of this book. We were committed to taking our ministry to people outside the church. And we were also committed to the truth that every believer is gifted and is to be equipped to use what he or she has for the ministry. We understood the application of those truths to mean that those we won to Christ would, in turn, need to become involved in winning their friends and colleagues and establishing them in Christ.

Our commitment to seeing these truths worked out thrust us into a dilemma. We discovered that the people we were bringing to Christ were worlds apart from the "cultures" of the existing churches. Those new believers who did cross over and integrate into them found they had, in the process, destroyed their lifelong network of relationships with friends and family. Their opportunities for outreach virtually ceased to exist because of the cultural distances involved. But if they tried to survive without a body of fellow believers, they would not only be barren, they would be malnourished and vulnerable to every kind of spiritual danger. It dawned on me that we were really dealing with a problem of form and function.

There were no forms in existence that would enable the people we were reaching to exercise the function of becoming established in Christ and, at the same time, fulfill the function of taking Christ to their friends and families. So we worked together for years, searching the Scriptures for guidance, until we managed to create appropriate forms that enabled us to fulfill the functions of edification and evangelism in that context. Indeed, we have learned that keeping those two functions vital and alive requires perpetual vigilance. The very forms we create have the perverse tendency to quickly lose their original usefulness and take on secondary meanings of their own. But that, I learned, is the inevitable dynamic that constantly goes on between form and function. The Bible is filled with both illustrations and warnings to this effect.

Form and Function in the Bible

In Exodus 18 we find Moses with a problem on his hands. He was spending all day, every day, attending to the needs of an endless line of people. Everyone in that camp of over a million people with an argument to resolve would come to him. It was killing Moses, and the people were getting poor service. His father-in-law, Jethro, had a suggestion. He said, "What is this you are doing . . . ? Why do you alone sit as judge, while all these people stand around you from morning till evening?"[10] Jethro suggested that Moses divide the work and then delegate it to honest, competent men. Moses did this. He appointed a body of judges. He thus created a form to accomplish a critical function—maintaining justice.

This form outlasted Moses. It outlasted Israel and lived on to become a Jewish institution. Forms do that.

This body of judges reappears in Ezekiel 8. By this time God had sentenced Israel to judgment. In this passage He is explaining, through Ezekiel, why He had passed such a terrible sentence on His people. He took Ezekiel into a chamber. It was filled with idols, and its walls were covered with obscene things. There, in the middle of that chamber, was that body of seventy elders Moses had inaugurated some five hundred years earlier. They were all there, and Jaazaniah was occupying Moses' seat. Ezekiel had been given a look at the thought life of Israel's leadership. God was saying, I have to judge this nation because of its judges. They have become perverse! What irony!

That form of seventy elders survived the Assyrian and Babylonian captivities and reappeared intact. Five hundred years later, when Jesus appeared on the scene, there it was. It was known as the Sanhedrin. Jesus described it thus: "The teachers of the law and the Pharisees sit in Moses' seat. So . . . do everything they tell you. But do not do what they do, for they do not practice what they preach."[11]

In Jesus' day, that form that had served Moses so well had taken on a life of its own. It had also taken on a new meaning. It existed primarily to provide seventy men with prestigious positions in the Jewish community. This becomes apparent in the account of the raising of Lazarus. An irrefutable miracle of this magnitude was perceived as a threat by the Sanhedrin. They said, "If we let him go on like this, everyone will believe in him, and then the Romans will come and take away both our place and our nation."[12] Jesus was a national security risk. He was a risk to the status quo. He had to be killed.

There are a number of similar illustrations of the interplay between form and function in the Bible. All of them teach the same lessons. Function calls for form. Form is the pattern an action assumes. We need forms. But once forms are created, they tend to become virtually indestructible. They live on and on. Functions are easily lost. When forms survive their intended function, they acquire new meanings of their own. They become a part of the tradition of a culture. They acquire an authority of their own. Then it becomes heretical to even question an established form.

Jesus Versus the "Tradition of the Elders"
In Jesus' confrontation with the "Tradition of the Elders," we have another very significant example of the interplay among form, function, and meaning. When Jesus appeared, He faced a five-hundred-year-old religious institution that was controlled by a few elite teachers of the Law. They claimed faithfulness to the laws of Moses and saw themselves as the guardians of the truth God revealed through Moses and the prophets.

The origins of this institution probably traced back to about the year 586 BC when Nebuchadnezzar liquidated the Kingdom of Judah. He destroyed the Temple and deported the majority of the Judahites. These Judahites carried their portable possessions, including the books of the Law and of the prophets, with them into exile in Babylon. In exile they began to meet to read and discuss the Scriptures. That was the birth of the synagogue. They first met in their homes and then, as the Persian government permitted, they constructed permanent meeting houses.

About seventy years later, in 520 BC, a remnant of the exiles was allowed to return to Jerusalem. Ezra was among them and Nehemiah soon followed.

The exiles knew why they had gone into captivity. It was right there in the writings of Amos.

> For three sins of Judah,
> even for four, I will not turn back my wrath.
> Because they have rejected the Law of the LORD
> and have not kept his decrees,
> because they have been led astray by false gods.[13]

The prophet Ezekiel singled out another sin that was apparently especially grievous—"they utterly desecrated my Sabbaths."[14]

The Judahites went into captivity because they had become idolaters, with all the immorality and injustice that that implies. But the root cause, said Amos, was that they had "rejected the law of the Lord." The neglected Sabbaths stood as a symbol of this rejection.

Those who returned to Jerusalem tried to restore some semblance of what they once were and had. They wanted to make sure no such calamity would ever befall them again. Ezra led the way. "Ezra arrived in Jerusalem in the fifth month of the seventh year of the king. . . . Ezra had devoted himself to the study and observance of the Law of the LORD, and to teaching its decrees and laws in Israel."[15]

Some of the returning exiles had no sooner arrived in Jerusalem than they began to gravitate back into idolatry. But Ezra was not lacking in tenacity. He got all the people to assemble in the square and read the Scriptures to them: "He read it aloud from daybreak till noon. . . . And all the people listened attentively. . . . They read from the Book of the Law of God, making it clear and giving the meaning so that the people could understand what was being read."[16]

Ezra sent readers to the surrounding towns, and they came back to Jerusalem with the populace in tow. There they listened for days on end as Ezra himself read from the Book of the Law of

God. Ezra read, rain or shine, and the people listened. They had had enough of captivity. Apparently Ezra got his point across—we dare not get away from the Scriptures. Let's make sure everyone hears and understands them.

It was following this return to God's Law that the Tradition of the Elders was developed, apparently in an attempt to explain and codify every detail of conduct. During the four hundred years of silence between the Old Testament and the New, several schools of scribes came and went. They assumed the task of explaining and interpreting the 613 laws of Moses in such specific terms that there would never be any ambiguity as to what constituted a violation. Thus they sought to build a fence of regulations around the Mosaic laws so that they would stand inviolate.

This took some doing. It required some fifteen hundred regulations just to protect the sanctity of the Sabbath. Is it a violation to collect eggs on the Sabbath? Well, that depends on why you are raising the chickens. If it is for the eggs, collecting them is work and is thus forbidden. But if it is for their meat, the eggs are secondary and you can pick them up. What about killing a scorpion on the Sabbath? No, that would be too much like hunting. And on it went.

These regulations had been passed on orally and are referred to in the New Testament as the "Tradition of the Elders." The big question was, what would Jesus do with it? Would He honor it?

This was the real question that lurked behind the many questions Jesus was asked by the Pharisees and teachers of the Law.

- ◆ "Why do You eat and drink with tax collectors and sinners?"
- ◆ "Why are You doing what is unlawful on the Sabbath?"
- ◆ "Is it right for us to pay taxes to Caesar or not?"
- ◆ "Why don't Your disciples live according to the Tradition of the Elders instead of eating their food with unclean hands?"

Jesus repudiated the Tradition of the Elders. He had no other choice. What had started out with Ezra as an honest, careful interpretation of Scripture had evolved into a system that trapped people in falsehood. He said, "'[Your] teachings are but rules

taught by men.' . . . You have let go of the commands of God. . . .
You nullify the word of God by your tradition that you have handed
down."[17]

Jesus proves that their professed fidelity to Moses doesn't
even exist.[18] They think they are gaining eternal life by diligent
study of the Scriptures, while ignoring Christ Himself who is
the centerpiece of the Scriptures.[19] Jesus said, "Your accuser is
Moses, on whom your hopes are set. If you believed Moses, you
would believe me, for he wrote about me."[20]

Jesus did not, could not, adopt a "live and let live" posture
with the teachers of the Law. Their teachings stood as an obstacle
to faith. He said, "[You] tie up heavy loads and put them on men's
shoulders. . . . You shut the kingdom of heaven in men's faces."[21]
The truth of the gospel could not coexist with the Tradition of the
Elders. The Man Jesus could not coexist with it either. It was that
set of laws that justified His execution. How fitting that His death
rendered all traditionalism, for all time, null and void.

Form and Function and the Early Christians

In chapter 7 we explored at length an undercurrent of tension
that ran through the entire New Testament narrative. That tension is related to this matter of form and function that we are
discussing here.

In spite of Jesus' aggressive confrontation with the teachers
of the Law over the Tradition of the Elders (which was soon to
become known as the Mishnah), and His decisive victory accomplished by His death and resurrection, that first generation of
believers was not immune to its power. The Apostle Peter's scruples against entering Cornelius's house did not come from what
Moses wrote. Peter said, "You are well aware that it is against our
law for a Jew to associate with a Gentile or visit him."[22] That law
won't be found in your Old Testament!

The elders in Jerusalem had the same difficulties. They were
aghast that Peter "went into the house of uncircumcised men and
ate with them."[23]

It is sufficient here to add a single comment. Just as Jesus
had to deal with the traditionalism of the teachers of the Law
because it was an *obstacle to repentance and faith*, the early

church had to deal with it for the sake of *the purity and mobility of the gospel.*

We all think we know what the gospel is and are convinced our favorite presentation of it is the pure stuff. It's not that simple. In the previous chapter we saw how difficult it is to preserve the purity of the gospel. That subject was the battleground over which the book of Galatians was written. Any add-on to grace by faith is an impurity. "You want to receive Christ? Fine, pray this prayer, and throw away your cigarettes." Even our little formula prayer can be an add-on, not to mention the cigarettes. That prayer is not what delivers a person from the dominion of darkness and brings him or her into the Kingdom of the Son. Submission to Christ does.

An impure gospel is an immobile gospel. It is not well received when extra requirements are included. As we examined the Acts 15 account of the Jerusalem Council, we noted that James summarized this point with the statement "We should not make it difficult for the Gentiles who are turning to God."[24] In the Epistles we find that the traditionalism that preserves dead forms impedes the gospel. Time and again the writers chide and admonish us not to succumb to such things. We read the Apostle Paul's words on the subject:

> See to it that no one takes you captive through hollow and deceptive philosophy, which depends on human tradi-tion. . . . Since you died with Christ to the basic principles of this world, why . . . do you submit to its rules: "Do not handle! Do not taste! Do not touch!"? . . . Such regulations indeed have an appearance of wisdom . . . but they lack any value in restraining sensual indulgence [which is the real issue].[25]

The volume of Scripture given to this issue of rules and regu-lations being imposed on believers is in itself a statement to its importance. Romans 14 and 15 deal with it. It is one of the primary threads that runs through the First Epistle to the Corinthians and the letter to the Galatians. The reason for such prominence is clearly stated in Hebrews 5:11–6:3.

People who are hung up on the elementary truths do not mature. The normal thing for a believer is to go on, to grow to where he or she can teach another. But people who never manage to pick their way out of their traditionalism consign themselves to perpetual spiritual infancy. Part of the maturing process is to have the latitude necessary to have "trained [oneself] to distinguish good from evil."[26] Traditionalism tries to do that for us. It says, "We know what's good for you. Just follow these rules." In so doing, it becomes *an obstacle to spiritual maturity*.

If in the interplay between form and function form survives while the original function is lost, the original meaning is also lost. Dead forms, cut adrift in this manner, are the stuff traditionalism is made of. And traditionalism is an opponent of truth.

In 2 Kings 18 we find an interesting example. As background, remember that on one occasion while Israel was wandering those forty years in the desert, God punished them for disobedience by causing an invasion of poisonous snakes into the Israelite camp. People were bitten and began to die. They appealed to Moses, who, instructed by God, had a bronze replica of the snake made and put on a pole. People who had the faith to turn and look at the form were healed. The snakes disappeared and the crisis passed. The bronze replica had served its function and could be discarded. But it wasn't.

Eight hundred years later, in Hezekiah's day, the bronze replica was still around! It had been given the name "Nehushtan" and had become an idol to Israel. Hezekiah "broke into pieces the bronze snake Moses had made, for up to that time the Israelites had been burning incense to it."[27] The function had long since disappeared, but the form remained, serving an extremely different meaning.

Traditionalism eclipses truth. We have seen how,

- ◆ In the gospels it was *an obstacle to repentance and faith*.
- ◆ In the book of Acts it was *an obstacle to the purity and mobility of the gospel*.
- ◆ In the Epistles it was *an obstacle to spiritual maturity*.

That doesn't leave very much untouched.

CONCLUSION

In this chapter we've been talking about the danger of being controlled by dead forms, forms that have lost their meaning but continue to live on. We have seen that the antidote is to make sure we are clear on the essential functions of the ministry, and make sure they are being done. This is an important but ignored dimension of church renewal. Who among us is not concerned about renewal? We had better be concerned about it, as even the most faithful among us are never more than a step away from mediocrity, or worse. The origin of any true renewal is, of course, Christ Himself. When we seek Him, we find Him. We come away from Him purified, because we cannot possibly be comfortable in His presence in our rags. Most experiences of renewal, however, are terribly short-lived. We can count on our fingers the occasions in history where renewal endured to result in permanent, significant change. Most often, we enjoy the warmth of the encounter like the passing of the sun, and then fall back into our old sheep paths. That is because we stop short. Renewal must include an honest appraisal of our actions. It is sustained by keeping the essential functions for God's people in focus, and being willing to sacrifice those forms that have lost their meaning.

This is a delicate subject. We have the freedom and the responsibility to change. We must, if we are to preserve the truth. As one friend put it, "You have to change to stay the same!" But it is so easy to get carried away in our zeal for change. Then we destroy. Certain things must change. Others must not. Wisdom is knowing which is which. Aleksandr Solzhenitsyn, in his memoir *The Oak and the Calf*, says, "Those who change the course of history are the gradualists, in whose hands the fabric of events does not tear."[28] I hope, by the end of this book, we'll have some criteria that will enable us to judge which is which.

CHAPTER NINE

New Boundaries
for the Church

▼

O ne lesson that comes through in our discussion of history and of form and function is that the church has constantly tended toward narrowing. With every redefinition, we exclude a bit more. Like arteries gradually shutting down, it becomes increasingly difficult for life-giving truth to get through. This has gone on throughout history, and the trend continues to this day.

The effect of narrowing is that we labor under self-imposed restrictions. We are restricted in our understanding of Scripture, and subsequently we are restricted in understanding God's people. One great need today is for us to return to Scripture to get a fresh reading on our bearings. We need to rediscover what the Bible has to say about God's workings, about the place His people have in those workings, and about the nature of ministry. It's amazing how much the Bible does say about these things, but it is equally amazing how consistently we ignore it and look to other sources for guidance in what to do as God's people.

OUR DIMINISHING BIBLE

As we have traveled through history, and as we go through life, we lose parts of our Bible here and there along the way. I have identified some of these losses in the course of this book, but there are others. To illustrate what I mean, let's imagine this square to represent the sum total of God's revelation to us in the Scriptures.

This square is limited in size, because the Bible doesn't tell us everything. It can't. The story of the Bible is an eternal story, which has no beginning nor ending. Consequently, Genesis 1 is not really the beginning of things, it's where our story begins. A lot of things are already going on. God, of course, is there in His diversity as Father, Son, and Holy Spirit. His Kingdom is there, and a fall has already occurred. Satan is on the scene, together with his angels.

The Bible doesn't attempt to explain the origin of these things. They are assumed. They are obviously, verifiably there. And the Bible doesn't bother to tell us much about eternity future. We are given some shadowy glimpses into what's in store for us and for creation. These glimpses fascinates us. But we are just going to have to wait and see to really understand.

So the Bible gives us what we need to know for now. What an amazing thing: a book from God containing all we need to know about life and godliness! The Apostle Paul said, "All Scripture is God-breathed and is useful for teaching, rebuking, correcting and training in righteousness, so that the man of God may be thoroughly equipped for every good work."[1] Apparently, God didn't waste any words. We need every bit of it.

But as we have seen in the course of history, many truths of the Bible have been placed beyond our reach. And we have continued the process. We are attempting to live life and participate in God's purposes while using less than God has revealed to us. The following are a few examples of what I'm talking about.

The Church Fathers

As the Church Fathers attempted to cope with the various pagan philosophies that threatened the church from without and the heresies that were popping up from within, they resorted to establishing a hierarchical structure as their solution. "Hierarchy" comes from two Greek words meaning "rule by priests." Thus, in doing this, our Church Fathers neatly and permanently divided God's people into two castes: laity and clergy. We have lived with this caste system ever since, even though the Bible teaches otherwise.

The Reformation

We have seen how the Protestant Reformers, striving to define a popeless church, approached the matter from two dimensions. They didn't seem to have much difficulty defining the church in universal terms. But when they asked the question "How do we know a local church when we see one?" they created some problems that we have inherited.

One example is the Reformers' treatment of the sacraments. Previously the pope had served as the unifying factor for the church. He defined the church. Since all the Reformers rejected the authority of the pope, a replacement symbol was needed. It is significant that the sacraments—particularly baptism and the Lord's Supper—are included in virtually all of their definitions. But do they belong at all? Is that why the sacraments were given to God's people? Is it baptism that makes a church a church? Is that why the Lord's Supper was instituted? The sacraments were not given to define the church for us. And whenever we impose a second meaning on something in this manner, its true significance is diminished or even lost.

Another neglected aspect in the definitions is the sending dimension of the people of God. Since the Reformers defined the church, with a few exceptions, as being a place where certain activities occurred among certain people, the traveling expressions of the people of God, such as the apostolic team, were omitted. The ministry of every believer in the world was also left out. Thus another piece of our Bible was placed beyond the reach of practice.

Theological Systems

We cannot do without theology, as theology in its broadest definition is the study of God in relation to the world. Every believer should be giving himself or herself to this pursuit.

Our problems come when we think we have it all figured out. We put it into writing, and that's the end of it. At whatever point we might stop, it's too soon! Paul says, "The man who thinks he knows something does not yet know as he ought to know."[2] Theology by nature is dynamic because it deals with an infinite God who is moving through history. A theological system is at best an attempted snapshot of what we manage to see and learn about Him at a point in time. There is nothing wrong with trying to get those snapshots. What is wrong is when we commit ourselves to a single picture, as if it contains all there is to be known about God. John Calvin spent his life revising his *Institutes*. We spend our lives studying them. But if he were still alive, he would probably be working on another revision, according to the growth of his own understanding of God and His ways.

So our theological systems can result in another narrowing of God's revelation. One can almost guess the theological persuasion of a person by looking at his Bible to see which parts are worn, and which are not.

Denominational or Organizational Distinctives

Most denominations and Christian organizations can trace their origins back to a particular issue or insight that the founders considered to be important enough to make the focus of their attention, and that of their followers. We saw how the Puritans originated around the idea of being a model of Christian virtue. Their mission was to become knit together as one in Christian community, and thus be as a "city upon a hill."

The organization I am with, The Navigators, was founded on the simple idea that one person can help another know Christ and make Him known. Dawson Trotman, the founder, spent his life teaching and practicing this truth of spiritual multiplication. Every organization and every church I know of has distinctives that greatly increase its effectiveness.

Distinctives bring focus to action, and thus are very powerful.

Their weakness lies in the flip side of focus: the tendency to ignore other truths of great importance that bring balance. So we can lose another part of our Bible because of a narrow focus on our distinctives. This is one more reason why one part of the body needs every other part just to be complete.

Culture

Culture can further reduce the perimeters of what we allow ourselves to see in the Scriptures. We all read our Bibles through the lens of our culture.

Over the past few years I've been working on a project that has brought together original biblical research from people of over forty different countries. We collected about one thousand pages of work on a range of topics. As we digested their work, I was struck again and again by how much culture *does* color what a person sees. The Japanese saw in their Bibles the importance of harmony, or *shalom*, and the prominence of nature. According to one paper, Jesus must have been of the Kikuyu tribe. A Finn chided the Westerner for ignoring the Unseen Reality, and so on.

We all peer through cultural lenses, and none of us can see very well through them. We need one another even to understand our Bibles properly.

The Familiar Sheep Paths

I know I have diminished my Bible even as I have grown in my familiarity with it. Occasionally, I buy a new Bible to get away from all the notes I've written in my old one. So I begin to mark up the new one. A couple of years later I compare the old copy with the new. To my dismay I find that my new discoveries, noted in my new Bible, have already been recorded in my former copy! I think many of us have a familiar sheep path worn through our Bibles that we enjoy following each time we read it. And we miss the rest.

Summary

So our Bible is truncated. We swear allegiance to all of it, but we operate within certain confines within the whole. God's revelation ends up looking like this:

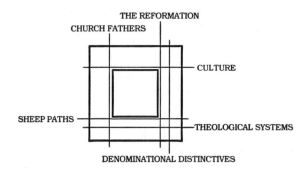

What remains of the Bible, unaffected by our exclusions, is just not ample for the demands of this hour.

OUR NARROWED UNDERSTANDING OF THE CHURCH

That we have in fact suffered this narrowing process can be illustrated by examining two statements we make repeatedly about the church. Both statements are usually made with all the confidence of someone who is uttering sacred writ. The two statements are as follows:

- ◆ The local church is God's primary means for accomplishing the Great Commission.
- ◆ Parachurch groups were raised up to do what the local churches should be doing, but aren't.

What do we mean by that first statement, "The local church is God's primary means for accomplishing the Great Commission"?

What other means does God have at His disposal in drawing people to Himself? Well, there are many. He uses His creation.[3] He uses calamity and judgment.[4] He uses the Old Testament prophets,[5] rulers, and historical events.[6] He uses His Word,[7] the Holy Spirit,[8] and His people.[9] Now, which of these is God's "primary" means?

Well, we reply, that's not what we're talking about. We're talking about accomplishing the Great Commission. That has to do with His people. So what we mean by the statement is, of all the forms of ministry Christians get involved in, what goes on in the local church is primary.

But we're still in trouble. Is not the diversity in the body God's idea? The apostle writes, "There are different kinds of gifts . . . different kinds of service . . . different kinds of working, but the same God works all of them in all men."[10] And did he not say, "There should be no division in the body, but . . . its parts should have an equal concern for each other"?[11] Are we making value judgments and comparisons between different members of the same body? Well, we reply, that's not what we mean either.

When it gets down to it, the phrase is usually intended to mean the following: "There is no other authoritative structure in the New Testament for doing God's work other than the local church. Any work of the church must be under the headship of local, recognized spiritual leaders." This quotation came from my notes from a lecture. It could have come from any number of sources, as this position is common. In a similar vein, people will say, "I believe in the local church." That sounds simple enough, but what they often mean, but leave unsaid, is, "I don't believe in anything else."

Our difficulties, at this point, lie in the fact that our entire discussion is based on assumptions we have picked up along the way in the course of church history, rather than on the Bible. The Reformers, remember, struggled with the question "How do we know a local church when we see one?" Since the "church universal" was too abstract to do anything with, their practical definition of the church inevitably had the local church as its starting point. Today we still tend to view the church through an exclusively local grid. This has a debilitating effect on the local church. A church that sees its own appointed leaders, staff, or majority vote as the sole source of spiritual leadership becomes an increasingly inward-looking church. Without the cross winds of other spiritual leadership, it ends up talking to itself. It will lack the range of vision and the experience needed to break out into the world.

The second statement, "Parachurch groups were raised up to do what the local churches should be doing, but aren't," reflects the same problem. It has its origins in the same ecclesiology as the first.

This ecclesiology begins by asking the question, "When is a church a church?" Our answers usually describe the church as consisting of believers who meet in a certain place where certain things happen. There is corporate worship, teaching of the Word, the sacraments, and there is leadership. A certain structure is implied.

Since these are not the central activities of parachurch ministries, they don't fit readily into our commonly accepted ecclesiology. So, we reason, such groups aren't really church. Come to think of it, we're not sure what they are! So, for many, a cloud hangs over this whole issue of parachurch. Parachurch and paramedic—handy to have around at times, but make sure it's a real doctor who does the surgery on me!

To say the parachurch groups exist because the local churches aren't doing the job again reveals the limitations of our prevailing understanding of God's people. It reflects the assumption that a really good local church is supposed to be doing everything. But any local body that attempts to do everything will simply fail in critical aspects. That is because a local body, like an individual believer, is a part of a greater whole. A local body needs to understand its sphere of ministry, its contribution—and the limits of that contribution—if it is to be effective.

We made a major mistake when we first admitted the term *parachurch* into our vocabulary. How can one part of a body be "para" to the other parts? This awkward division of local and parachurch structures has resulted from our narrow understanding of the church. This narrowing costs us dearly, as it leaves the unbelieving world in no-man's-land.

WHAT IS THE CHURCH?

How we answer this question is determined to a large degree by the questions we use as we begin our search. If we begin by asking, When does a particular group of people cross the line and constitute a church? our thinking will pursue a certain path. The problem with such a question is, it's just not big enough. If we are to come to an adequate understanding of God's people, we must begin with questions that embrace the whole of God's workings in the world. We need to see ourselves as God's people, in a broad context. Our understanding of the church needs to be large enough to embrace all the Bible has to say about what it means to be His people, and what it means to be in the world. The breadth of our definitions must be dictated not by the institutional boundaries that circumscribe certain activities, but by the totality of our calling.

I believe there is a single truth that must lie at the heart of any adequate definition of the church. In essence, the church is *people who are indwelt by the Holy Spirit, who is transforming their character and giving them gifts they are to use for service. Every believer is to use whatever he or she has to serve one another—and his or her neighbors.* Most of the big passages that have to do with God's people in the New Testament revolve around this truth.[12]

Paul summarizes this in Ephesians: "We will in all things grow up into him who is the Head, that is, Christ. From him the whole body, joined and held together by every supporting ligament, grows and builds itself up in love, as each part does its work."[13]

So what's new? we ask. All this sounds familiar enough until we examine the implications of these passages. The verses may be familiar, but their practice is not. I believe there are four factors that must be present if we are to function as a church according to this definition.

Christ Must Be the Head

The Apostle Paul reassures the Ephesian Christians that "to each one of us grace has been given as Christ apportioned it. . . . [He] gave gifts to men." "All these are the work of one and the same Spirit, and He gives them to each man, just as He determines."[14] Notice that references to Christ and to the Holy Spirit are interchanged in these passages.

The Holy Spirit is the source of life for God's people. Without Him there is nothing. With Him, every believer becomes an essential, contributing part of the whole. There are to be no bleachers—no place to just sit and watch.

Christ is the Head—not the figurehead, not the chairman of the board. He is the "hands-on" Director and Orchestrator of all that goes on. He calls no board meetings, as there is no board. He deals, instead, with every member, every individual directly through the Holy Spirit. We all have the "mind of Christ."[15] This tells us a lot about what leadership is to be and what it is not to be among God's people. Leadership has to do with serving the body by exercising one's function. This does not negate the need for human authority among God's people, but it puts it into perspective. Nor does it rule out positions of leadership. It does mean those who occupy positions are not "the top." There is no "top." As Paul said, "Not that we lord it over your faith, but we work with you for your joy, because it is by faith you stand firm."[16]

The Body Must Live in Community

Another dimension of this truth is community. The body "builds itself up in love." *Koinonia*, as used for example by John, means "life in the family."[17] Body life is twenty-four hours a day, seven days a week, and embraces the full spectrum of our activities. As we go through life as believers, we are to attentively serve one another, encouraging one another toward godliness in every area. As believers formed themselves into identifiable bodies in the first centuries, their times of gathering were just the tip of the iceberg of their life together.

Our life as a family in God's household is critical to our going to the world. As we have previously observed, it is the unique nature of this life together that makes us light in the world.[18] Then as we allow ourselves to be scattered into the world, our need for one another becomes a matter of life and death. We will need like never before the care and support of our brothers and sisters.

There Must Be Diversity of Functions

The central truth we are discussing also takes us back to the matter of the diversity of functions in the body. Since we have already discussed this subject at length, it is sufficient here to call our attention to the fact that so many of the instructions given to believers in the New Testament can't even find their expression in the sanctuary, or on the premises of the church property. Some examples of these instructions include: "Offer hospitality to one another";[19] "Live in harmony with one another";[20] "Do good to all people, especially to those who belong to the family of believers";[21] and "Remember those in prison as if you were their fellow prisoners."[22]

When it comes to leadership functions, the same applies. Some find their expression more readily when God's people are gathered, while others are more naturally fitted for when they are scattered. The important thing to observe here is that it takes the whole list, as given in Ephesians 4, to equip people for ministry. It takes apostles, prophets, evangelists, pastors, and teachers.[23]

All of This in the Presence of the Unbelieving World
If our lives as God's people are to be lived out in full view of the world, we need to take conscious, deliberate steps to be sure this is happening. This calls for resetting the boundaries of our definitions of the church.

RESETTING THE BOUNDARIES

Perhaps the big difference in what we're saying has to do with where the boundary markers are being placed as we define the church. What is in-bounds? What is out-of-bounds? I am proposing that the boundary markers for the church should be determined by where the gifts and callings of God's people take them. If believers were encouraged and enabled to seize the opportunities God brings their way in the neighborhood and across society, and if they could proceed confident of support from others in the body, the church would be redefined. It would change from being a bounded set to being a centered set.

Bounded Sets and Centered Sets
What we are arriving at here is truly a paradigmatic change in the way we perceive the church. We are accustomed to defining the church within a certain circle. We work at clarifying who is in, who is out; what the leadership structure is to be and not to be;

what we believe and do not believe; which activities belong, which do not; and what behavior is appropriate and what is not. So the line between insiders and outsiders is clearly drawn.

Paul Hiebert of Trinity Evangelical Divinity School calls this kind of thinking "bounded-set thinking." That is, there is a boundary that sets the standard. One either qualifies or is rejected; it's pass or fail. What I'm advocating in this chapter is that we move from bounded-set thinking to what Hiebert refers to as "centered-set thinking" in our understanding of the church.[24]

In a centered set, what counts is how each member is moving in relation to the center. The focus is upon the center, and each individual is in dynamic relationship to it. Belonging, in this case, is not a matter of performing according to an agreed-upon profile, it is a matter of living and acting out of commitment to a common center. The focus is on the center and on pointing people to that center. Process is more important than definitions. Centered-set thinking affirms initiatives that would otherwise not find a place. It rewards creativity.

It is not that bounded sets are always bad and centered sets are always good. Boundaries do exist. Salvation is a bounded set. One is either in Christ, or not in Christ. Discipleship is a centered set. To be a disciple is to be constantly moving toward the center, which is Christ.

What we are talking about can be visualized by the following diagram.

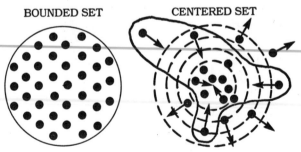

Source: PAUL HIEBERT

Bounded Set and Centered Set and the Church

This distinction is helpful in communicating some of what I have been saying in this chapter. To view the church from the perspective of the centered-set model opens the possibility for recovering its multiform nature, and thereby its mobility.

If we use this model, our understanding of what is the center must be very clear. The church is not that center. The center is the Head of the body. All members of the body are to function in relation to the center: Christ. If there is confusion on this point and we think of the church as being the center, we will find ourselves merely creating another bounded set.

We have described God's people as being people who are indwelt by the Holy Spirit, who is transforming their character and giving them gifts they are to use in serving their brothers and sisters—and their neighbors. To accept that description means accepting the idea that exercising our gifts and functions, according to the enabling of the Holy Spirit in response to needs and opportunities, will determine our boundaries.

Leadership and Authority in a Centered-Set Model

The reader could easily be thinking that what I'm advocating here would result in pandemonium, with everyone moving in whichever direction he or she pleases, doing whatever strikes him or her as a good idea at the moment. That *would* be pandemonium. We are a body, knit together by the Holy Spirit through our strengths and weaknesses and bound by love. We are all to "submit to one another out of reverence for Christ."[25] We need leadership. I think Ephesians 4:16 talks about leadership when it says we are "held together by every supporting ligament."[26] And there is authority. We're told, "Obey your leaders and submit to their authority."[27] Leadership and authority are inseparable, as one cannot exist without the other.

We will be discussing how to respond to these things in an orderly way in the final three chapters of this book, but the heart of the matter lies in what we have said about form and function. In the New Testament we saw how the ministry was accomplished by believers exercising certain functions. Form and structure followed, giving substance and permanence to their efforts. It is that process that needs to be repeated and reproduced, not the existing forms.

CHAPTER TEN

God's People in the Midst of Postmodern America

▼

I n the previous chapter we called for a redefinition of the church that defines it in terms of its functions rather than a prescribed set of structures and forms. We argued that the issue calling for such are definition is the urgent need for God's people to regain their mobility, the ability to take the initiative and go to our society with the message of Christ. We showed how the church refined its skills to attract people to "come to," but does not yet understand what it means to "go to." The church has yet to learn what it means to be God's people sown in the world, alongside the sons of the Evil One.

Thus, we continue to operate on two faulty assumptions. First, we assume we can get the world to come to us. Then, we assume that when they do come, we have what is necessary to meet their needs. These assumptions do hold true for a relatively narrow segment of our society. They work for some, but they do not hold true for the mainstream American. We underestimate the effects postmodern thought is having on society. In chapter 2 we described the direction our society appears to be headed. Our response as God's people—what we do and how we do it—must be appropriate to the contemporary need. In this chapter we will begin to explore what it will mean to regain the initiative.

Theoretically, we now have the space in our understanding of the church to accommodate the necessary mobility. This allows us to entertain a set of questions that, until now, were beyond our reach. They were beyond serious consideration. We can now ask, What is the task we face as we go to mainstream America? What are we getting into? What needs will we encounter? What will it require of us to meet them? What vehicles will be required to take us to where we need to go? Who is to do what? How might it look? What forms might our efforts assume?

We can summarize such questions in the following sequence:

◆ What do we face?
◆ What is the task?
◆ Who is to do it?

These three questions broadly outline the remainder of this book. The first one will be addressed in this chapter. To do so, we need to pick up where we left off in chapter 2. Recall how we moved from the past to the present in that chapter. Now we will project into the future our assessment of contemporary society. We return to this subject now because, if we hope to minister to people in ways that realistically deal with their particular needs, we need to bear in mind what they think, how they think, and why their behavior is what it is.

We ended our assessment in chapter 2 with the observation that our society is becoming postmodern.

POSTMODERN THOUGHT: WHAT IT DOES TO PEOPLE

Postmodernism? How can something be later than modern? Postmodernism identifies the breaking up of the Enlightenment consensus that real truth can be found by scientific processes, and that there is solid ground out there for rational people to stand firmly upon. We saw how the Enlightenment peeled apart truth and values, and consigned the latter to individual preference. Postmodernism completes the wreckage by dethroning truth. Truth is perceived as being relative and biased.

Allan Bloom's grandparents would have been described as

ignorant people by today's standards. Though his grandfather held only unskilled jobs, the family was spiritually rich because of its simple faith and practices. Bloom describes the gradual change in determining truth from his grandparents' day to the present:

> In the United States, practically speaking, the Bible was the only common culture, one that united simple and sophisticated, rich and poor, young and old . . . the very model for a vision of the order of the whole of things, as well as the key to the rest of Western art. . . . With its [the Bible's] gradual and inevitable disappearance, the very idea of such a total book and the possibility and necessity of world-explanation is disappearing. . . . Without the book even the idea of the order of the whole is lost.[1]

This loss of "the book" leaves people on their own, to create their own gods according to their own preconceptions. *Harper's Magazine* published a startling dialogue between two cultural critics that makes the point. The two critics are Neil Postman and Camille Paglia. From the dialogue—titled "She Wants Her TV! He Wants His Book!"—here are a few of Paglia's comments:

> People born before World War II can't understand those of us raised in the fragmented, imagistic world of TV.

> If you look at it from my perspective, popular culture is an eruption of paganism—which is also a sacred style. . . . [In] the great studio era of Hollywood movies in the 1930s and 1940s . . . Cinema then was a pagan cult full of gods and goddesses, glamour and charisma. . . . So it's not that the sacred has been lost or is being trivialized. We are steeped in idolatry. The sacred is everywhere. I don't see any secularism. We've returned to the age of polytheism. It's a rebirth of the pagan gods. . . .
>
> Judeo-Christianity never defeated paganism but rather drove it underground, from which it constantly erupts in all kinds of ways. . . .

I date the modern age from the first sound pictures in 1928. I call the twentieth century the Age of Hollywood.

Rather than your total secularization, I see the repaganization of Western culture.

You say TV is Dadaist in its random, nihilistic compilation of unrelated events. I say it's surrealist—because *life* is surreal![2]

As we saw in chapter 2, there is much more behind the shift than Hollywood and the TV screen, as Paglia suggests, but that is beside the point. What is significant is the fact that someone like Camille Paglia, who lays no claim to the Christian faith, makes the observation that we have returned to paganism, and *that's just fine with her!*

This has become a pagan society, and we have filled it with our gods. We will worship anyone who can show us a good time, whether it is by acting, singing, throwing a ball—or even preaching. Our offerings to our idols confirm our idolatry. The average baseball player earns four times as much as does our nation's president. (Of course, our idolatry is not confined to personalities.) So in this, Paglia is right. We are not godless at all. We have just changed gods.

THE NEW *STOICHEIA*

The gods people choose, whichever they might be, become their master. These gods invariably impose a set of controlling laws and boundaries. Pluralism, which is fast becoming a predominant characteristic of our society, is no exception. Pluralism is seen as the true spirit of freedom, proper for a dogma-free society such as ours. Relativism, a corollary to pluralism, leads us to think that somehow doubt is more noble, more intellectually honest, than belief. To really believe something, in this present context, is seen as bigotry and arrogance.

The problem with this reasoning is that it cuts both ways. If we cannot conclude that something is true or false, we lose our ability to think at all. How can we go on to point B if we are committed to the relativism of A? This is Allan Bloom's thesis in *The Closing of the American Mind*. His title is well chosen. By it he says that in our pursuit of openness, our minds have become closed. Relativism, the belief that there are no absolutes, no truth—and pluralism, the belief that whatever is "true for me," or "true for you," *is* "true"—are, in fact, ideas that are as enslaving as Zeus and Ares ever were. "What is advertised as a great opening is a great closing."[3]

There is nothing in this approach to truth that encourages, or even permits, the big questions: What is the purpose of life? Why am I here? Why is there suffering? What is the meaning of salvation? The postmodern person avoids such questions as being out-of-bounds. He or she is therefore left with no real basis for proceeding with even the mundane matters of life. "In the absence of any objectifiable criteria of right and wrong, good or evil, the self and its feelings become our only moral guide."[4] "Good" is what "feels good."

Life is hard when lived on this basis. On the personal level it is characterized by uncertain introspection. Am I doing what's best for me? Is life getting away from me? How long should I stay in this relationship? Questions like these tend to be consuming and paralyzing, because they lack an external framework. They revolve, instead, around the self. This search for "the good" is a road to bondage. Terms like *addiction, addictive behavior, compulsive behavior, dependency,* and *codependency* have become a part of our everyday vocabulary. Where these words were once seen as applying to immoral or criminal behavior, they now cover a broad spectrum from drugs and alcohol to caffeine, nicotine, amphetamines, and barbiturates. We are also beginning to realize we are confronted by a host of other addictions. Things like gambling, sex, shopping, eating, and exercise are being included among addictive behaviors.

The "pursuit of openness" to which Allan Bloom refers is also turning us into bigots. We are as prejudiced as we ever were at any other time in our history. We have merely put the shoe on the other foot. I have a friend who lost his position at Harvard University because, in a discussion with some students, he suggested that it might be worthwhile to look at homosexuality from the perspective of morality. Such an idea, fumed one of his accusers, is beyond consideration! Subjects such as sexuality, sexual differences, race, and other similar issues are so hot we don't even dare approach them with scientific research! In reverence to openness, we are forbidden to think.

LOOK OUT FROM BEHIND!

We who make up the church find ourselves swimming in this same soup along with the rest of society. Some of us attempt to keep our distance and to keep our children out of it, but eventually we all get wet. Our TV sets are on, we read the magazines, take the same courses under the same professors, and work in the same marketplace along with everyone else. Most of the time someone is trying to sell us something, with either a billboard, a commercial, or a phone call at dinnertime. Even if we don't buy the product, we unwittingly take on the images created by the advertising. Eventually it gets to us. How do we avoid picking up some of the values we have just been describing?

Of course, we have already been affected. Pollster George Gallup, Jr., makes this very clear. "America has the soul of a church but the heart of a hypocrite. . . . Americans say they are extraordinarily attached to religion. . . . But while this attachment to religion is wide, it's not very deep. Ethically, there is little difference between the way people who claim belief and the minority of non-believers conduct their business or academic practices."[5]

He goes on to say that Americans are "'biblical illiterates.' We revere the Bible but we don't read it."[6] He indicated that only half of those claiming to be Christians know who preached the Sermon on the Mount. One third of the teenagers do not know the significance of Easter. "The 'boomers' (born from 1946 to 1964) . . . too often . . . are attending, but not believing." For them, "the Golden Rule of the New Testament has come to mean either 'Don't bother anyone' or 'Let them do their own thing.'"[7]

In the articles quoted above, Gallup also says that 40 percent of Americans attend church or synagogue weekly, but that only 10 percent of Americans would not be included in the above descriptions as biblically illiterate and ethically indistinguishable from the majority. That would mean that 75 percent of our church members are nominal indeed.

Barna and McKay are even stronger in their analysis. They say, "Rather than adhering to a Christian philosophy of life that is occasionally tarnished by lapses into infidelity, many Christians are profoundly secularized, and only occasionally do they respond to conditions and situations in a Christian manner. Recent research shows that many Christians are especially vulnerable to the worldly philosophies of materialism, humanism and hedonism."[8]

After giving a message at a missions conference in a Bible church not long ago, I was conversing with some of the leaders. One of the group was responsible for the curriculum for the youth. She observed, "Truth is those things all the religions of the world have in common." I was so surprised, so caught off guard, I could not reply. Had I been sufficiently quick-witted, I would have responded that the major religions hold nothing in common by way of belief. So if that is the criteria, there is no truth.

A multitude of similar illustrations exists. One that is more extreme appeared in a *Newsweek* magazine article titled "A Time to Seek." The article reports a return to religion among the baby boomers. That's the good news. The bad news is the state of many of the churches these people are returning to. Market-driven as they are, their first concern is often to please the customer. One pastor, *Newsweek* reports, "has been criticized for using the word humankind because it leaves out animals and plants."[9] This is pantheism!

In a sense, this subject, the effects of relativism and pluralism on the church, is beyond the scope of this book. But it is such a critical issue, I feel I would be negligent if I failed to address it. Perhaps the world will get to us before we get to it. In some situations this is already the case. And wherever it is the case, we have nothing left to offer. "If the salt loses its saltiness . . . it is no longer good for anything."[10]

SO, WHAT DO WE FACE?

There must be two parts to our answer to this first question. First, we must take into account the fact that we live in a society that is, in many ways, reverting to paganism. Biblical beliefs and values are becoming increasingly foreign to popular thought. Second, we face the internal threat of having our foundations compromised in our efforts to be relevant and attractive as God's people.

CHAPTER ELEVEN

The Task Before Us

▼

We have seen the pervasiveness of paganism in our society, the challenge ungodly philosophies present to the Christian underpinnings of our way of life. Now we come to another challenge, which is also the second of our three questions: What do we need to do if we are to fruitfully serve the people of our society with the message of Christ?

This question takes us back to our thesis, which can instruct us at this point. We'll review it here.

◆ God's people are in the world to bear witness to the world. We are to live among our unbelieving neighbors, serving them, revealing Christ to them.

◆ This ministry depends upon every believer. We are all to use whatever we have to serve God by serving our sisters and brothers, and the unbeliever.

These two truths are timeless because, as we have seen, they are central to the biblical description of what God's people are to be about in this world. Given our contemporary cultural context as I have just described it, these two truths can be translated into two statements of task. Our task is as follows:

- ◆ To bear witness to Christ in such a way that truth prevails over relativism.
- ◆ To empower believers to witness and bring healing to broken people at the scene of the need.

BEARING WITNESS TO CHRIST

How does one bear witness to Christ among people who believe that one truth is as good as another? Where do we begin? What do we say? Will not our statements of confident belief in God and His purpose for the world be dismissed as ignorance, arrogance, or dogmatism? In this section, we will see that the answers to these questions depend upon how we go about witnessing.

The pressure is on us to join the spirit of the day. "Is it not more fitting," asks Lesslie Newbigin, playing the devil's advocate, "that we adopt the attitude of a humble seeker after truth, keeping an open mind, ready to listen to all that comes from the varied religious experience of the human race? Is it not more honest as well as more humble to stop preaching and engage rather in dialogue, listening to the experience of others and offering our own, not to displace theirs but to enrich and be enriched by the sharing of religious experience?"[1]

Of course, such an abdication to pluralism is incompatible with the central message of the Bible: that God has revealed Himself, ultimately in Christ. If we believe this to be true, we are compelled to witness to that truth. This witness involves two elements: the message and the messenger.

The Message

Jesus said, "I am . . . the truth."[2] How strange! I puzzled over these words for years. Is not truth, I would wonder, propositional by nature and expressed as concepts? Why, then, did He not say, I *teach* the truth, or, I *bring you* the truth? But no, He said, "I *am* the truth." He, the Person, Jesus of Nazareth, *is* the truth! He is our message. Our message is not a system of thought, a set of propositions to be matched and compared against another set. Our message is a Person. We make *Christ* known. Paul, the apostle, said, "I resolved to know nothing while I was with you except Jesus Christ and him crucified. . . . My message and my preaching were not with wise and persuasive words, but with the demonstration of the Spirit's power."[3]

The Hindu is the ultimate pluralist. Within Hinduism there's room for monotheism, polytheism, agnosticism, and atheism. The roots of Hinduism reach back five thousand years, perhaps into the Canaanite religions of the book of Genesis. There are striking similarities between the two. The Hindu feels his system works. Human suffering is interpreted by the karmic cycle of reincarnations. You reap what you sow. Your present karma is what you deserve from your previous incarnations. There's room in the system for sixty million gods and for ideas that diametrically oppose one another. There's only one place where Hinduism draws the line: on dogmatism. Hinduism rejects absolutes.

E. Stanley Jones spent most of his life in India evangelizing among Hindus. In his autobiography, *A Song of Ascents*, he describes the discoveries he made along the way.

Jones relates a conversation he had one evening with a judge that was key to bringing the issue into focus for him.

"I asked him," wrote Jones, "'Who is a Hindu?' He replied, 'Any good man is a Hindu—you are a Hindu.' I asked, 'Where does the Hindu end and the non-Hindu begin?' He replied, 'You can believe anything and still be a Hindu.' 'Yes,' I replied, 'anything from atheism to pantheism. But where does the Hindu end and the non-Hindu begin?' He thoughtfully replied, 'You can believe in anything and still be a Hindu, provided you don't reject the rest.' Here," observes Jones, "he put his finger on the genius of Hinduism—it is syncretic; it takes in everything, provided it doesn't 'reject the rest.' But," he reflected, "I belonged to a Person who presented himself as the Way, the Truth, and the Life. How could there be a 'right way' . . . in the eyes of the Hindu judge?"[4]

Jones describes his own pilgrimage to fruitfulness among Hindus. He said, "I knew my message was Jesus Christ, but since I had been brought up conservatively, I was out to defend everything I held. I was on the defensive. My theology was neat and tied up with a blue ribbon—unchanging."[5] Then it dawned on him. To debate system against system, religion against religion, was a losing proposition. It was his word against theirs. But since "the

Word became flesh," everything Jesus taught was a fact within Himself. He didn't just *bring* the good news; He *was* the good news. The gospel lies in His Person. Philosophies point to truths; Jesus said, "I am the truth."

So, Jones concludes, "I am free to listen to others and hear what they say their faith is doing for them . . . knowing that in the end Jesus will occupy the center. I am free, for I don't have to defend Jesus. I have to present him, and he is his own defense."[6]

Jones's discoveries run very parallel to our own, as we worked to understand how to communicate Christ to the educated Brazilian in the 1960s and 1970s. Through trial and error and searching the Scriptures for answers, we learned that people who avowed their unbelief and disinterest in religion would nonetheless willingly work their way through the Bible with us week after week. But we had to disentangle Christ from the wrappings we customarily present Him in to gain that hearing.

We learned that if our explorations revolved around just two questions, there would be fruit. The questions were: Who was Jesus? and, What does He want of me? We learned we didn't have to debate ideologies or theologies. We didn't have to win the argument. We could count on the superiority of Christ to carry the day. This does not mean that because we have Christ we possess all truth. "There is a true sense in which we are—with others—seekers after the truth. . . . When Christians affirm . . . that Jesus is the way, the true and living way, . . . they are not claiming to know everything. They are claiming to be on the way, and inviting others to join them as they press . . . toward the day when we shall know as we have been known."[7]

The Messenger

The messenger we are concerned about in this chapter is the "insider." It is the believer who, like good seed, has been sown in the world; in a neighborhood, in the marketplace—in short, across society. How does he or she exercise this function of being a witness that successfully confronts relativism with truth? We would do well to keep the following six principles in mind as we live our lives as messengers to the world.

1. To be a messenger of Christ is to participate in spiritual warfare. People are in slavery to the world systems wherever they find themselves. The Bible says they are under the control of Satan, ruler of this world. The problem is not just that they don't want to understand, it's that they cannot: "The god of this age has blinded the minds of unbelievers, so that they cannot see the light of the gospel of the glory of Christ."[8]

Only spiritual weapons are of any use in this spiritual war. The Apostle Paul writes, "For though we live in the world, we do not wage war as the world does. The weapons we fight with are not the weapons of the world. On the contrary, they have divine power to demolish strongholds."[9] Thus the real confrontation takes place in the unseen reality.

What are these weapons? Prayer, God's Word, and a Christ-like life.[10] Through our obedient use of these resources, the Holy Spirit accomplishes the supernatural work of rescuing the person from the dominion of darkness and bringing him or her into the Kingdom of the Son. Conversion is a divinely orchestrated jailbreak!

2. Communicating Christ involves incarnation, not just information. Where the gospel is concerned, the medium is the message: "The Word became flesh and lived for a while among us. We have *seen* his Glory . . . full of grace and truth."[11] Jesus was the Incarnation of God Himself. He was God in flesh and blood. He incarnated the Father. We are to incarnate His message. The Apostle Paul said, "Our gospel came to you not simply with words, but also with power, with the Holy Spirit and with deep conviction. You know how we *lived* among you for your sake."[12] In other words, the people Paul went to both heard the message and saw it lived out in his life.

To incarnate means to give flesh to, or to embody. As such, it is a fitting word to describe the way we are to live life. When the writers of the Epistles describe believers in an unbelieving world—as does Paul in the following passage—that was where they placed their emphasis: "For you were once darkness, but now you are light in the Lord. *Live* as children of light . . . for it is light that makes everything visible. . . . Be very careful, then, how you *live*—not as unwise but as wise, making the most of

every opportunity, because the days are evil."[13] We are to *live*
incarn_____ _____ _____ _____ becoming, in Christ,
is to b_____ _____ _____ _____ are not called
upon _____ _____ _____ _____ there is power
in bei_____

3_____ _____ _____ _____ ust an event.
One o_____ _____ _____ _____ it all at once.
We w_____ _____ _____ _____ th a friend or
acqua_____ _____ _____ _____ e whole message _____ _____ _____ _____ ople are ready
for th_____ _____ _____ npt results in
polar_____ _____ ow to never let
them _____ _____ and would-be
mess_____ _____ and often give
up fo_____ _____ does not have
to be _____

J_____ _____ ss. He told the
apos_____, _____ orked for. Oth-
ers have done the hard work, and you have reaped the benefits
of their labor."[14] When we do reap a quick harvest, it is because
someone else has already been working that field. It is not always
harvest time, but it *is* always time for something—planting, cultivating, watering, or harvesting.

It is a relief to realize we are only part of a process. I ask God
to use me to move every person I meet a step closer to Christ.
Sometimes I reap, but far more often I do not. Sometimes I witness verbally, but more often I do not.

4. The messenger adapts to the hearer, not vice versa. In
chapter 8 we observed that we all need a certain amount of ethnocentrism just to hold life together. We adhere to a set of customs,
traditions, and behaviors because we need the sense of belonging
and predictability that they bring us. We also saw how the Christian community tends to create its own subculture much in the
same fashion and for the same reasons.

Christians often have the additional tendency to arrive at personal convictions on relative matters of behavior—and then universalize them. This is the essence of legalism. Legalists decide
what is right or wrong for themselves in such matters, and for

everyone else! They say, this is bad for me—so no one else should do it either.

Our inherent ethnocentrism can in itself stand as a barrier between ourselves and those we would reach with the message of Christ. But when that barrier is heightened by our Christian subculture, the distance often becomes insurmountable.

The people we are sent to as witnesses live within their own customs and traditions. We need to be aware of that fact and concede to their ways rather than expecting them to adapt to ours. This is the way of love. Love for the unbeliever motivated the Apostle Paul's statement, "I have become all things to all men so that by all possible means I might save some."[15] His instructions to the believers in Corinth reveal that he expected the same attitude on their part: "If some unbeliever invites you to a meal and you want to go, eat whatever is put before you without raising questions of conscience."[16] This ability to set aside one's personal scruples to give preference to the other person allows the gospel to come to that person in its purity, unencumbered by nonessential requirements.

5. *Witnessing among unbelievers is a team, or body, effort.* Liberty, freedom, and the rights of the individual are foundational values of this nation. This freedom has been abused and translated into *individualism* in the negative sense. The necessities of pioneer life contributed to this. In frontier days, might was right. One had to be self-reliant and resourceful just to survive. With the passing of the wild West, these same attitudes were carried into the boardroom. Our early millionaires got there because of their extraordinary self-confidence. They got there first and brooked no interference from others, not even from the government. Success has come to be measured in terms of possessions and power.

We repeatedly attempt to carry this individualism over into ministry. It is always disastrous. According to the Bible, we weren't made to go it alone. God has distributed some gifts to each of us and has withheld others. No one has all the gifts. The things He has withheld are as important to us as the things He has given. Our deficiencies make us interdependent on one another, and therein lies our strength. There is power in working together in unity. Jesus prayed, "May they be brought to complete unity to let the world know that you sent me."[17]

This unity and interdependence is a statement that confronts people with the truth of Christ.

It is also very practical. Who among us has all the abilities, the experience, sufficient time, and the energy to plan, initiate, prepare, and sustain a ministry single-handedly? We can't do it alone, but with a little help from our friends the part we do have will be significant. There is great power in a small team of two or three couples, or any small group of Christians who have learned to complement one another according to their abilities. Together they constitute a vehicle that can carry them into the mainstream of our society, like a small boat that can take them where they are to do their fishing.

6. *We guide people to Christ through the Scriptures.* Late in the first century a tract was written for the expressed purpose of giving people what they needed to know so that they "may believe that Jesus is the Christ, the Son of God."[18] It contains roughly 18,800 words, takes a couple of hours to read—and a lifetime to fully understand. I'm referring, of course, to the Gospel of John.

But in this society that boasts of speedy service and fast foods, we have cut the content of our gospel down to a couple hundred words that fit neatly into a booklet that can be both read and explained in twenty minutes. Granted, there are certain times when such a summary is exactly what is needed. People who are on their way to Christ, who understand parts but not the whole of the message, often need nothing more than an explanation of this sort to complete their journey. The problem lies in the fact that many of the relatively small number of Christians who do share their faith equate such a summary with the whole gospel. It is the only resource they have ever learned to use. But how, may I ask, can our modern, pagan friends get a proper look at Christ when we approach them with such an abbreviated message?

I have learned to sit down with an unbelieving friend, or small group, and over a period of time just read that first-century tract and talk about it. As the person Jesus emerges, faith becomes plausible. Then, as the truths of Scripture are reinforced by loving relationships, faith becomes irresistible. This may happen over a period of weeks, or it may take months.

This is so simple, yet so powerful.

Conclusion: The prevalence of relativism should not intimidate us. I don't believe it makes people more difficult to reach. We just need to be aware of its control over people's minds. Our resources are ample, as we have seen.

As we work at translating these concepts into practice, there will be failures and successes. We will learn as we go. Forms and methods will emerge as we repeat our successful experiences. These will be relevant, to be sure, because they will be produced within our particular context. But they should not be regarded as permanent, because the next situation we find ourselves in may be quite different.

EMPOWERING BELIEVERS TO WITNESS AND HEAL

Our ministry is to broken people, as that is the only kind of people we will find. We are all broken, it's just that it's harder for some of us to admit it. Jesus said, "It is not the healthy who need a doctor, but the sick. . . . For I have not come to call the righteous, but sinners."[19] And He said, "I tell you the truth, everyone who sins is a slave to sin."[20] That catches us all. Everyone has been enslaved and debilitated by his or her own sin.

But our problems run even deeper than that. God warns us repeatedly in the Old Testament that "he punishes the children and their children for the sin of the fathers to the third and fourth generation."[21] We may protest that this is unjust. But in reality that's the way life is. How much have you carried over into your life from your parents that you determined not to take with you? Brokenness is compounded from one generation to another.

We have seen how terms such as *addiction, abuse, dependency, codependency,* and *compulsive behavior* have become a part of everyone's vocabulary. The secular therapist appears to have found a permanent place in many people's lives. The primary function of the secular therapist is to help people feel good about themselves. They help people keep enough emotional capital in their bank to be able to make it until their next visit. As one therapist comments, "Ultimately I think people want to know they're O.K., and they're looking for somebody to tell them that. . . . What people really need is self-validation."[22]

The secular therapist serves as something of a priest over the individual in his or her quest for wholeness, and their sheer numbers in this society are something of a measurement of how needy people really are.

The biblical counselor should not be equated with the secular therapist in this discussion. A counselor who does his or her work on the basis of biblical principles is really what the Bible calls a shepherd, or pastor. There is a great need and much opportunity for people gifted and trained to be modern-day shepherds, both within the body and without.

The people we go to are going to need healing. They are dealing with the cumulative effect of several generations of broken relationships. They have been abused, ignored, bought off, and so on. What are we going to do about problems like these as people meet Christ? Are we going to help them find a good therapist? Or are we going to find a good program for them someplace? Will we send them to a church? To a specialist? Or will we help them ourselves? The last option, for us to help them ourselves, seems the least likely of the lot. But it could be the only option many would have access to, and often proves to be the most powerful. Let me give you an example.

Antonio's spiritual birth was a long, painful affair that dragged on for almost two years. We would meet together every few days, and we would have wonderful times exploring the gospel. But he could not bring himself to submit to Jesus Christ. He had some sexual habits he wasn't sure he could live without. He made attempt after attempt to change his behavior, but his efforts always ended in failure.

Gradually, he began to understand he was getting the cart before the horse. He was attempting to change so that he would be acceptable to God. Finally, he gave himself to Christ as he was, and asked Christ to change him. I breathed a sigh of relief, but the next eighteen months were even more difficult. Antonio's problems didn't go away. I continued to spend hours with him, and on his way home from our visits he would often stop and visit a prostitute. He would be back to see me the next day, full of remorse. This happened over and over. I taught him everything I could find in the Bible on sexual behavior, and prayed for him daily. But there was no improvement. Finally I gave up. Antonio seemed beyond my help.

One verse heightened my sense of failure: "Do not be deceived: Neither the sexually immoral nor idolaters, nor adulterers . . . will inherit the kingdom of God. And that is what some of you *were*. But you *were* washed."[23] They had been delivered!

I puzzled over how believers in the first century, with no professional training, could achieve such profound transformations among the morally sick, and how powerless my own work was by comparison. Since Antonio's problems were the rule rather than the exception among the people we were reaching, I began to wonder if our ministry even had a future.

How did they do it back then? That they did it at all is proof that it can be done, I reasoned. So I went to the Scriptures with this question: What are the essential elements of true spiritual change? What are the dynamics?

I was looking for something simple. It would have to be simple, because those first-century Christians had managed profound changes without the benefit of modern psychology. What I learned follows.

THE DYNAMICS OF SPIRITUAL TRANSFORMATION

The following six factors, essential to personal spiritual transformation, work together to produce true inner change. These factors interrelate roughly in the sequence I describe here. The cycle needs to be continuous to accomplish permanent change. Any change, any deliverance from a particular habit or attitude, results from an ongoing interaction among these factors. There will always be areas in our lives as we progress toward the likeness of Christ that will be undergoing this process of deliverance.

Experiences of Life
Everyday life is our schoolroom. Experiences are at the center of all change. They can be positive experiences, or negative ones.

The Apostle Paul relates, "We were under great pressure, far beyond our ability to endure. . . . But this happened that we might not rely on ourselves but on God, who raises the dead."[24] An experience led to a discovery. The result was increased capacity. We "rejoice in our sufferings, because we know that suffering produces perseverance."[25]

Reflect back on your own life. What major changes have you undergone? Are these changes not experience-related? Of course they are. Change does not occur in a vacuum. Godliness is not gained on a mountaintop. I will not learn to be faithful to my wife as long as she and I are marooned on a deserted island. Experiences reveal what I really am and confront me with my needs. So experiences will be at the center of any change.

EXPERIENCE

We all have experiences all the time, but few of us seem to benefit or learn from them. We can either be trained by the experiences of life, or they can leave us bruised and bewildered. This brings us to the second essential element in the process of change.

The Scriptures

If we did not have the Scriptures, we would be unable to make sense of our experiences. The psalmist said, "Your word is a lamp to my feet and a light for my path."[26] Using the same metaphor, Jesus adds, "Everyone who does evil hates the light, and will not come into the light for fear that his deeds will be exposed. But whoever lives by the truth comes into the light, so that it may be seen plainly that what he has done has been done through God."[27] The revelation of Christ, both incarnate and written, illuminates the way to truth, and to true deliverance. So the Scriptures are also essential to personal transformation.

THE
SCRIPTURES

EXPERIENCE

Too often the best our modern therapist is able to do is make us feel better about our problems, or rearrange them in such a way that we find them easier to live with. It is not deliverance at all, it is accommodation. This is because the therapeutic attitude, many times, never gets beyond the self. "In the absence of biblical truth, the meaning of life for most Americans is to become one's own person, almost to give birth to oneself."[28]

The Bible confronts us with truth about ourselves. It is like a mirror that, like it or not, reveals us as we are. James writes, "But the man who looks intently into the perfect law that gives freedom, and continues to do this, not forgetting what he has heard, but doing it—he will be blessed in what he does."[29]

This passage indicates that it is possible to have experiences, to understand them through the light of the Scriptures, and still make no progress. We can be like the person "who looks at his face in a mirror and . . . goes away and immediately forgets what he looks like."[30] Something is required of us.

Humility

Humility is foundational to the next element in spiritual transformation. In the words of James, "Humbly accept the word planted in you, which can save you."[31]

There can be no deliverance without humility. That is because we cannot really be honest without it. How difficult it is to say, "I did it. I was wrong!" But these words take us out of our darkness and into the light. To say them brings us out into the open, before God and man. And once we are there, we can be healed. *Confession* and *repentance* are synonyms for what we have just described. So the process of change proceeds.

There is great power in humility. It is the prerequisite for all spiritual understanding, for learning and for repentance. It opens the way for confession. It can heal not only the soul, but also the body! David writes about it:

> When I kept silent,
>   my bones wasted away
>   through my groaning all day long.
> For day and night
>   your hand was heavy upon me;
> my strength was sapped
>   as in the heat of summer.
> Then I acknowledged my sin to you
>   and did not cover up my iniquity.
> I said, "I will confess
>   my transgressions to the LORD"—
> and you forgave
>   the guilt of my sin.[32]

After looking at what the Scriptures say about humility, we come away with the impression that humility is conditional to resolving almost any problem we will ever face. God said,

> This is the one I esteem:
>   he who is humble and contrite in spirit,
>   and trembles at my word.[33]

God's response to people who humble themselves apparently knows no limits.

The Holy Spirit

Not long ago I had a conversation with a young Muslim. We were talking about knowing God, and it was apparent that this was something he greatly desired. At one point in the conversation, he asked, "What can I do to control the enticements of my flesh?" He wanted to clean up his life.

Everything I have described to this point about spiritual transformation is possible, to a degree, for this young Muslim. He can seek to understand his experiences in light of the Scriptures. It would be conceivable for him to humble himself and admit his wrongdoing. He would benefit from that, and life would be better for him. But he would never really experience transformation. And I told him so.

The Holy Spirit is the one who divides Christ's way from all other ways. Almost any religion or philosophy will help bring order, or structure, into a person's life. But the Holy Spirit brings life itself. "Love, joy, peace, patience, kindness, goodness, faithfulness, gentleness and self-control"[34]—these are ours through Him.

Many Christians don't get much help from the Holy Spirit. That is because He *can't* help us until we stop relying on our schemes for self-improvement. Once that matter is dealt with, He can move in on our situation, "for it is God who works in you to will and to act according to his good purpose."[35] Both the desire to change and the ability to do so come from Him.

So we add the Holy Spirit to our diagram.

Self-Control

Jesus said, "Everyone who sins is a slave to sin." But He then added, "If the Son sets you free, you will be free indeed."[36]

We are not condemned to spend our lives in a losing struggle against our old addictive behaviors. As we gain insights into our needs through the Scriptures, and as we respond with humility, the Holy Spirit empowers us to act differently the next time the old patterns come around. It is a self-control born of the Spirit, "for God did not give us a spirit of timidity, but a spirit of *power, of love* and of *self-discipline.*"[37] The slavery to the old behavior is over, and we are free to make different choices.

Not that these new choices are painless. Nor does a single victory mean deliverance. There will be pain and ambivalence as we give up our favorite set of chains. But freedom becomes more satisfying with every victorious choice. So we make a circle.

But our process is still incomplete.

What happened to Antonio? During our last week in Brazil, Antonio took me for a long walk. More than a decade had passed since the day I had given up on him. He just wanted to tell me how he was doing. I had heard from others that life had come together for him and that he was being unusually fruitful in bringing many of his unbelieving friends to Christ. But he wanted to be sure I knew of two major victories that had him very excited. He had been faithful to his wife and honest in his business!

Antonio had experienced the transformations I have just described. But I have not yet mentioned what I believe to be a major element in his transformation. I believe this next one is fundamental to the process.

One Another

As my colleagues and I struggled with this matter of inner transformation, Hebrews 3:13 appeared to offer a key to much of what we were looking for: "But encourage one another daily . . . so that none of you may be hardened by sin's deceitfulness." This verse implies an intense (daily) accepting environment, where sins could be an open topic of conversation among believers committed to one another.

We went to work to discover how to translate this verse into practice. The resulting form, which we called "cell groups," became the basic unit of our ministry. They were simply a nucleus of up to a dozen people—couples and singles—who helped one another translate biblical truth into everyday living. They also proved to be an ideal environment for ongoing witness among peers. We learned that a small group will soon become unhealthily introspective if it neglects this dimension of corporate and individual witness.

A while after I had given up on Antonio, he and his bride became a part of a cell that consisted of three other couples. All four couples were struggling as much as Antonio was, but they pulled each other out of their very serious problems. I suspect their mutual weakness was a part of their power.

What could this little group of struggling Christians do for Antonio that I was unable to do? James 5:16 gives the answer: "Therefore confess your sins to each other and pray for each other so that you may be healed." This honesty, this mutual spiritual support, heals. It just does.

Dietrich Bonhoeffer, in commenting on this subject, said,

> He who is alone with his sin is utterly alone. It may be that Christians, notwithstanding corporate worship, common prayer, and all their fellowship in service, may still be left to their loneliness. The final break-through to fellowship does not occur, because, though they have fellowship with one another as believers and as devout people, they do not have fellowship as the undevout, as sinners. The pious fellowship permits no one to be a sinner. So everybody must conceal his sin from himself and from the fellowship. We dare not be sinners . . . so we remain alone with our sin. . . . The fact is that we *are* sinners! . . .
>
> In confession the break-through to community takes place. Sin demands to have a man by himself. It withdraws him from the community. The more isolated a person is, the more destructive will be the power of sin over him. . . . In the darkness of the unexpressed it poisons the whole being of a person.[38]

Thus for our illustration to be complete, we need to place it in a context of true community.

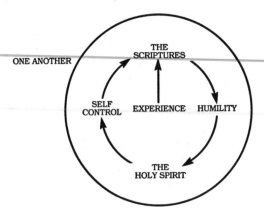

One of the great unresolved challenges facing us as God's people today is to discover how to be true community in this transient, on-the-run society of ours.

CONCLUSION

In this chapter we have assessed some of our contemporary philosophical trends for the purpose of understanding what we will face as we communicate the truth of Christ in this society. We then went on to define the task—what needs to happen—in light of the trends. We now proceed to our final question, Who is to do this work we have been describing?

CHAPTER TWELVE

Recovering Our Mobility

▼

I n the previous two chapters we dealt with two questions. First, we examined the question, What do we face as we go to our society as witnesses to Christ? Then we answered the question, What is our task? A natural objection to what I have said so far would be, "Who is supposed to do all this? You are calling for skills we don't have and time we cannot spare." That's probably true. We cannot accomplish what we are talking about if we only work within the confines of our familiar forms and priorities.

We saw in chapter 4 how the church of the first century was multiform in its expressions and how the combined effects of the gathering and scattering of God's people—together with the "traveling functions"—resulted in the expansion and penetration of the gospel. If we have any hope of accomplishing the task before us today, we must recover that kind of mobility.

We have been talking about the essential functions of God's people, some of which are missing. We need to keep our focus on the functions and not get caught up in the forms, which need to vary with the situation. Form, remember, follows function. This means we begin, not by conceiving of a structure and then organizing it into existence, but by identifying what needs to be done (the function) and then empowering the appropriate people to give themselves to the task. We, indeed, have the freedom to bring what is necessary into existence. The purpose behind much of what I've written in this book is just that, to demonstrate that we have both the freedom and the responsibility to do what the hour demands.

Two primary functions need to be recovered at this time. We will call them *the apostolic team* and *the local expansion of the gospel.* Both terms are imperfect, but I trust that as we progress in this chapter the concepts will become clear. As we explore the meaning of these two functions, we will be answering the question of *who is to do this work* we have described.

THE APOSTOLIC TEAM

In chapter 4 we examined the subject of apostles and the apostolic function quite thoroughly, and in chapter 7 we got into it again. We recognized the obvious uniqueness of the original twelve and of the Apostle Paul. We also saw that a number of other people were identified as apostles: Barnabas, Apollos, Timothy, Epaphroditus, Silas, etc. They were simply people who had been sent out on a mission, "sent ones" exercising a function. They occupied no special position, nor did they command any unique authority.

We are often uncomfortable with the word *apostle* today— probably because of the way it has been abused. For some, it conjures up images of special positions of authority, or of succession from the original twelve. Such notions have no part in our definition. Because of such abuses I would use a synonym if one existed. *Missionary* comes close, but popular usage has rendered it even more misleading to the concept I wish to communicate. We use *missionary* to describe everyone from accountants to mechanics, if they happen to be on foreign soil. There's nothing wrong with that, but it renders the word inappropriate for our use. That's why we're using the word *apostle*.

Of the apostles, we know most about Paul and his activities with his team. They were aggressive, focused pioneers who crossed cultural and social boundaries for the sake of the gospel.

They did not preach and run. They lived with the fruit of their efforts until those they reached could not only care for themselves, but also assume the holy trust of keeping the gospel flowing among their compatriots. *That* is the function we need to recover! In fact, if we do not, we will fail this generation.

Where, we ask, is this needed? Shut your eyes and throw a rock! Wherever it lands would probably be a good place to begin. This country has cultures and subcultures; inner cities, suburbs, and rural towns; social classes and professional circles—many of which go unaffected by the message of Christ.

A contemporary apostolic team might consist of two or three appropriately gifted people who have the experience and skills for this kind of ministry. Their objective would be to fulfill the command of Matthew 28:18-20, to *go* and make disciples by introducing people into the resources that are theirs in the Father, the Son, and the Holy Spirit. Something new will be born, but how it will look will follow no predetermined blueprint. Forms will be developed as needs, felt and unfelt, are met. New fellowships or bodies will take shape, or existing fellowships will be enhanced.

For these reasons, an apostolic team of this sort needs the freedom and authority necessary for their task. If they find themselves controlled by preset specifications, or by the rulings of their sending body, they will sacrifice the integrity of their work. It is extremely difficult for people who have only had local experience to grasp the complexities of keeping the gospel pure while taking it from one culture to another.

It is interesting to observe the dynamics of the relationships between the apostolic teams and the various groups of local elders in the first century. What they did would not necessarily be normative for us, but it is instructive. While they did not operate independently of one another, neither held final authority over the other. Where there was disagreement, as in Acts 15, the apostles and the elders, representing the mobile and the local expressions of God's people, met together to unsnarl their differences. The two operated in dynamic relationship with one another.

As time progressed, a voluntary, mutual submission developed between the sets of leaders. Galatians 2 is an illustration of this dynamic. The Apostle Paul states, "I went up again . . . in response to a revelation and set before them the gospel that I preach among the Gentiles. But I did this privately to those who seemed to be the leaders. . . . As for those who seemed to be important—whatever they were makes no difference to me; God does not judge by external appearance—those men added nothing to my message."[1]

"Those men" were no less than James, the brother of Jesus and elder of the Jerusalem church, Peter, and John! Paul in this passage articulates his indifference toward externals such as position and his deep commitment to mutual submission to his peers. It was this spirit that preserved the freedom of form the church needed to go where it needed to go and do what it needed to do. Our contemporary "apostolic teams" will need similar attitudes, and similar freedom.

THE TASK OF THE APOSTOLIC TEAM

The apostolic team faces four major requirements to carry out its mission. They can be summarized as follows.

Rapport
Until rapport is established, there can be no communication. People need to say, "I want to hear what you have to say." One reason Paul went to the synagogues was because he knew he would find people there who were interested in hearing what he had to say. Some would scoff, others would not believe, but always some would say, "We want to hear more."

One of the difficult challenges we face today is to find a way to gain a serious hearing among those we need to reach. We try a lot of things, but often our tactics are not conducive to establishing rapport. Recently, I talked to a person who had visited over three thousand homes for the purpose of offering a witness. He had had eight decisions. This person was not lacking boldness or zeal. He just wasn't getting rapport. The front door was the wrong situation for the kind of people he was approaching. They weren't ready for a serious discussion of life-and-death issues with a stranger.

So the first task of an apostolic team is to discover where and how they can gain a serious hearing with the people they are intent on reaching.

Comprehension

The second challenge facing an apostolic team is to get their hearers to truly comprehend their message. Comprehension says, "Aha, I understand what you are saying!" True understanding must occur if there is to be genuine faith. Jesus said, "When anyone hears the message about the kingdom and does not understand it, the evil one comes and snatches away what was sown."[2] We can get decisions, lots of them, without comprehension. But we cannot get transformed lives, because such decisions are not born of faith.

Comprehension takes time and perseverance. It usually requires more than words. Paul said, "Our gospel came to you not simply with words, but also with . . . deep conviction. You know how we lived among you for your sake."[3] We do not commute to and from this kind of ministry. It means going to and living among. That is because people cannot *see* enough of the gospel to truly comprehend it if we only make our appearance to witness or when it's time to study the Bible.

Relevance to Life

When the people in Thessalonica understood the gospel, they "turned to God from idols to serve the living and true God."[4] Conversion is the beginning of a transforming process. It is a turning from, and a turning to. How could it be less, as conversion results in the Living God taking up residence in one's life? He lives among those who are His. There is no way that life can go on unaltered when there is true conversion.

But as we saw in the previous chapter, this transformation doesn't progress on its own. It requires great sustained effort on the part of the message-bearers.

We see this as Paul goes on to remind the Thessalonians of how "we dealt with each of you as a father deals with his own children, encouraging, comforting and urging you to live lives worthy of God, who calls you into his kingdom and glory."[5] Making the gospel relevant to life for new believers is work, not unlike that required to raise your own children. But if we stop short, if we are negligent or unwilling to give of ourselves in that way, the entire effort will ultimately prove to be irrelevant. The dramatic changes in lifestyle will not occur in the new believers—and if these do not occur, the gospel will not continue to expand beyond that first nucleus. It will be dead-ended; there will be no reproduction. In that case, the apostolic team would have to again put themselves through the laborious task of foundation laying.

Colaborship

Colaborship is when those coming to Christ reach sufficient maturity to where they, in turn, become message-bearers. Paul says, "The Lord's message rang out from you not only in Macedonia and Achaia—your faith in God has become known everywhere."[6] This brings us back to our thesis. Every believer is to carry his or her part in the ministry. Where this does not happen, the ministry is dead-ended. And given the size of the task—a lost world to reach—that is unacceptable. Paul wrote to the believers in Philippi, "Hold out the word of life—in order that I may boast on the day of Christ that I did not run or labor for nothing."[7]

Each of these four stages of ministry will represent a "frontier experience" for us. Since the traveling expressions of the church have largely fallen into disuse, we have little contemporary experience to go on. The recovery of this function will require creative experimentation, trial and error, and perseverance. It will not be easy.

The closest parallel to this function today is the missionary team that goes into a place to begin something new. (Some parachurch work also approximates what I am describing.) With no institutions to maintain or positions to fill, missionaries in such circumstances have no alternative but to set out to gain a hearing with the people they are seeking to reach.

I have had that experience on several occasions in my lifetime and always found it extremely demanding. Particularly difficult are the very early days in a new effort where the immediate task is to gain a hearing, to establish rapport.

As I launched into my first experience, my already substantial discomfort was heightened by a statement Jesus made: "Every plant which my heavenly Father has not planted will be pulled up by the roots."[8] I understood by this that I could go out there, generate a lot of activity, and begin to make things happen. I could even make things look good. But if those beginnings were not from God, they would not endure. This turned the whole effort into an exercise in faith for me. I had to take the initiative, but I realized that my basic posture before God had to be one of submission and dependence.

The way Jesus referred to the Twelve in His prayer to His Father served as another similar guidepost for me. Whenever He talked about those men He referred to them as "the men you gave me out of the world." If Jesus viewed the people He ministered to as being gifts from the Father, how much more should I have the same attitude! So I began to pray constantly that God would put me in touch with the people in the city that He was already drawing to Himself.

Paul's starting point was the synagogue. As we already observed, it was a place of rapport. He could go there and people would want to hear what he had to say. The church is not today's equivalent. The church is for believers. Paul's preaching would decimate the synagogues—a fact that did not seem to bother him much. He was bearing a message of life and death to lost people.

On one occasion, after some months of relatively fruitless struggle, we realized we needed to create our own equivalent of the synagogue. What was needed was a safe place where people who did not believe could listen, take a look, and walk away to think about what they heard without fear that someone would buttonhole them before they got out the door.

The form we created was what we called the "open study." These studies were held biweekly in our home or some other neutral place and were led by the handful of young believers we had already reached. They were designed for people who did not believe and included no songs, no prayers, no jargon, no quick answers, and no calls for decisions. As those young believers realized that these sessions were indeed safe—that we would not invade the space the unbeliever needs to work through his or her unbelief—they increasingly brought their friends and peers

around. The studies were reinforced by steady social involvement—barbecues, soccer games, anything where people could
get a closer look at their Christian friends. It was the gospel
incarnated. The result was a "synagogue" of from forty to sixty
people in various stages of interest in Christ. We had our rapport. It became a simple matter then to invite those individuals
who were responding to take a closer look at Christ through the
Scriptures. It was very fruitful.

I describe this effort, not to offer it as a model, but as an illustration of the kind of innovation required to effectively field contemporary apostolic teams. We found that every step we took, at
every stage, required equivalent creative effort.

THE LOCAL EXPANSION OF THE GOSPEL

An apostolic team can go where a congregation cannot and make
things happen that would not occur by any other means. It enjoys
tremendous mobility. But it too is limited. Such a team can get
things started by laying foundations that can support much
future growth. But because the team members are outsiders,
they cannot really penetrate a society with the message. Only
one kind of person can do that.

We saw how Jesus likened us to good seed sown alongside
the sons of the Evil One. He also described us as salt and light.
The thing these metaphors have in common is that they are only
effective when scattered, or released. The believer is the insider.
He or she is the only one who can truly penetrate society. Three
times in 1 Corinthians 7 we find statements to this effect. In verse
17 it says, "Each one should retain the place in life that the Lord
assigned to him and to which God has called him." Then in verse
20 we read, "Each one should remain in the situation which he
was in when God called him." Verse 24 says virtually the same
thing a third time. According to these verses, even new believers
are already strategically positioned by God. They don't have to
go out and search for a place to minister. They are already in it.
To find their calling they merely need to open their eyes. Most of
us spend our lives moving about in the mainstream as we carry
on our businesses and live life in our communities. The question

is not, where can I go to find opportunity to minister? Rather, it is, how do I go about making the most of the opportunities that already surround me?

SMALL BOATS

As we have worked our way through the Scriptures in the course of this book, we have repeatedly been reminded of our interdependence on one another. We have seen that we have all been given gifts, but none of us has them all. So we need one another. Rarely does a lone believer manage to make the most of his or her opportunities as an insider. We all need help. The individual needs the reinforcement of a few other like-minded brothers and sisters. Together they can accomplish things that would be impossible if each tried to go it alone. As people team up in this way, they form a vehicle for ministry—a small boat. Together they can push off into the current of the mainstream and get to the holes where the fishing is the best.

There are fundamental differences between "fishing from a small boat" and working as an apostolic team, however. An apostolic team needs autonomy of action as it goes from the known to the unknown in the development of its ministry. Team members need to have the maturity and experience to be able to handle that freedom. The little nucleus that launches out in their small boat, however, has the opposite need. They will need constant coaching, encouragement, and support—and a safe place to dock when it storms. They have a high dependence on the body and its leaders.

Another major difference lies in the mode of ministry. The goals may be similar, but the methods are very different. Both need to achieve *rapport, comprehension, relevance,* and *colaborship* among those to whom they minister. The starting point for the apostolic team is usually among strangers. This means they need to aggressively open the channels of communication between themselves and the people they seek to reach. In contrast, those in the small boat have a limited number of fishing holes to go to—for example, a neighborhood, an office, or a network of old friends. To follow the analogy, the apostolic team fishes with a net or maybe even dynamite, while those in the small boat angle. True, you can throw a stick of dynamite into your neighborhood—once. Then you have to find another place to fish. The skillful angler catches fish without disturbing the pool. This is the challenge to those who fish from the small boat. They need to learn to minister in such a way that they avoid driving off people who do not immediately respond, while at the same time becoming increasingly attractive or alluring to those looking on.

The great advantage the people in the small boats enjoy is that they are already strategically positioned as insiders to a community. They should make the most of this advantage and work to preserve it. Preserving it implies keeping the network of friends and acquaintances they are reaching intact for as long as possible. This means that their task is more than just conducting an evangelistic Bible study in their neighborhood, although it will probably include such an activity. Their task calls for living among and being involved enough with people for Christ's love to be demonstrated. It is being an outpost community for people who are discovering Christ. And there is always the possibility that the outpost will become a new center.

WHAT WILL BECOME OF US?

In essence, what we have just said is that those among us who feel their function in the body is best accomplished "off campus" should be encouraged and enabled to do just that. But to think in these terms will require a paradigm change for some of us. It will mean a reordering of our thinking—away from being centered around sanctuaries, pulpits, pews, and clergy and to focusing on neighborhoods, offices, living rooms, laypeople, and our neighbors.

These are unsettling ideas. They raise a myriad of obvious, difficult questions. Those people in the small boats—where are they to learn to do these things? Where will they find the time, the energy? What about their other involvements in the church? How will they maintain their ties with the rest of the body if the center of their ministry is "off campus"? What about their children? In short, is this not a recipe for chaos?

It could be! But we are between a rock and a hard place. In the course of this book we have developed the thesis that God's people are in the world to bear witness to the world and that this ministry has been given to every one of us. If this is truth, we cannot simply acknowledge it as such—and then proceed, course unaltered, as if it were not so. It is our responsibility to bring practice into line with truth. But this is not simple to do. Truth ineptly applied can destroy. Even bad timing in attempting to implement a truth can do more harm than good. So the tension mounts. What are we to do?

The questions we have raised here are real—but they are not our real problem. There are answers to them. The real problem is the break with the known, the familiar, that these ideas represent. Few people enjoy change. I don't. I dislike moving from one house to another, buying a different car, or even altering my little habits that annoy my wife. I like to sit in the same chair at the table and sleep on the same side of the bed. I find it uncomfortable to give up something I know and do well to become a beginner in something unfamiliar to me. It is easier to go through life repeating known patterns.

If change comes hard even in trivial matters, we can be sure it will be difficult in matters of great importance. In matters of our faith we find ourselves in the context of several millennia of history. Over the centuries various major strands of traditions have defined themselves within the church. Each is meaningful to those raised in them. They are a part of the *sense of place* we talked about earlier. Thus, in our zeal to apply truth, we could easily leave many displaced persons—emotional refugees—in our wake. To bring about benign change, change that does not harm, is an art.

THE ART OF CHANGE

One of my colleagues pointed out to me that there are three basic approaches to change. There is change by revolution, change by reformation, and change by innovation.

Change by revolution is almost always more destructive than constructive. It is a revolt against the prevailing system. It seeks to put an end to that system and replace it with another. Everything stops while the old system is being dismantled and the new one is being put into place.

Bolivia has had more national presidents than it has had years of history as a republic. This fact in itself would explain its current economic woes. For a country, wealth is not money, it is the ability to produce. A revolution interrupts a country's ability to produce. The country falls behind, often never to catch up again.

It is hard to imagine revolution ever being a fitting approach to change in matters related to the Body of Christ.

Reformation has to do with attempting to fix an existing system. It is change by reordering what is there. We have the Protestant Reformation as an illustration of this approach. The records of history give us an abundance of information on what change by reformation can and cannot achieve. Great good was accomplished by the Reformers, but the pioneers of the Reformation did not envision the outcome of the various processes they set into motion. They did not want to "unchurch" themselves. Their vision was to reform the system of which they were a part, it wasn't to create a new parallel system. But that, of course, is not how it worked out.

We have to admit that reformation, as an approach to change, does have its place in the body. But innovation is probably a better word to describe our current need.

Change by innovation is accomplished as innovative people experiment and learn within the sphere of their own lives and ministries. As they learn through their experiences, others are able to pick up on what they are doing and carry the discovery process further. It is a seminal approach. It experiments and learns without imposing the discoveries on the rest. It does not insist that everyone and everything around it adopt the changes. It thus leaves what is already in existence intact.

PRINCIPLES OF INNOVATIVE CHANGE

Innovative change should be a constant among God's people. There is always so much to learn, so many unanswered questions, and so much "unoccupied land." Books have been written on change, and there will be many more. It is sufficient here to identify the few basic principles that innovative change depends upon.

Be Your Own Guinea Pig

It is relatively easy to come up with good ideas. And often, the longer we think about a new idea, the better it gets. It grows until it gradually takes over our minds. We talk about it and we find it makes sense to others. So the idea gains momentum. At that point we might even write a book about it. Karl Marx did that. His major work, *Das Kapital,* is an exposition of a set of ideas that never had stood the test of reality. If we could somehow pass a law that all ideas needed to be tested in the laboratory of the author's life before they got any further, the world would be spared most of its pain—and the information glut we now swim in would slow to a trickle.

Theology as a discipline is especially vulnerable to being perpetuated without being tested in the matrix of life. It can be passed from teacher to teacher, book to book, and mind to mind without ever being applied. But biblical truth, if it is truth, will stand the test of being helpful for building people up according to their needs. It will benefit people. It will change their lives.

While I was starting out in my ministry in Brazil, I received numerous invitations to speak to churches and organizations about the things I was doing. But I hadn't really done anything in that country yet. So I would decline. I feared that my ideas, untested as they were, were more likely to confuse than help.

I have tested these things I have written here, but nonetheless I write with apprehension, as the danger of confusing and misleading is still high. My prayer is that the reader will have the wisdom to judge the things I have said against the Scriptures, and then put them to the test of experience in his or her own situation.

The challenge to all of us is to learn from our experiences, to glean the lessons that are there for the taking. We do this by periodically taking time to reflect on what is happening and to summarize the progress in our understanding. In time we will find that our discoveries will begin to fit together. As they do they become increasingly useful to ourselves and to others.

Be Patient; Every Idea Has Its Time

Years ago I observed an exchange of correspondence between two people who lived on separate sides of the world. The exchange produced great frustration for both correspondents, and unfortunately permanently marred the relationship between the two. Since I was a friend to both parties, I was informed of the reactions on both sides.

The opening salvo from the person on the other side of the world was a well-reasoned call for change based on some obviously true observations. The letter was directed to his supervisor. This person, in his response, could not deny the validity of the observation and the call to change. The problem was, he was already overwhelmed by the things on his agenda. In fact, the organization he was working with was in crisis, wondering if it even had a future. He did not think to explain this in his reply. Rather, he attempted to respond to the issue with a superficial explanation as to why things were the way they were in the area under discussion.

Upon receiving this response, the first party easily picked it apart and sent a second salvo that resulted in both sides taking offense.

The lesson I learned as I watched this was that any idea, no matter how significant or how true it might be, must wait its day. As a result, I made three decisions that I have attempted to follow in my own efforts at bringing about change.

- ◆ Observe. Learn all you can from the things going on around you. Act on what you learn. Do what you understand to be right in your own life and ministry. But don't universalize your own personal experiences.
- ◆ Commit what you're learning to God. If He wants the things He's teaching you to go further, let it be His move. Leave it to Him to open the doors for you.
- ◆ Give thanks no matter what happens. If you have opportunity to influence, accept it. If you don't, give thanks.

In that case, God has probably spared others from things they don't need!

Accept Rejection of Your Ideas

New ideas will encounter opposition for the reasons we have already indicated. Someone has described the sequence as

- ◆ Rejection
- ◆ Toleration
- ◆ Acceptance
- ◆ Embracing

Often an idea will be rejected, if for no other reason than because it's new. People need time to think about something new. But after it has been around awhile, it is tolerated. Then the attitude moves from negative to positive as the idea gains acceptance. Finally, it is embraced. This means others have made it their own. Often the period between the initial rejection and the embracing is measured in years. That leaves plenty of time for criticism, disagreement, and opposition.

Honest criticism should be welcomed, as it can only serve to test and improve your ideas. Ideas must be able to survive the test of honest criticism. If they can't, they probably shouldn't. Criticism puts our ideas back on the drawing board. It sends us back to the Bible. We come out strengthened if we can receive criticism openly.

There also needs to be space for disagreement. There's room for more than one position on most issues. To positively accept disagreement is to leave others with the space they need to think for themselves. Most people resist being pressured to think a certain way.

Opposition can be fatal to new ideas History is filled with examples of truths snuffed out by their opponents. But even opposition constitutes an opportunity. It brings faith into the picture. If an effort is not of God, we shouldn't want it to succeed. And if we truly leave the fortunes of a matter in God's hands, the opposition constitutes no obstacle to Him. He can preserve what is valuable.

Summary

In essence, what I'm saying here is that our own egos are our most dangerous enemies in this matter of innovative change. If we allow our sense of personal worth, or of our identity, to get wrapped up in our ideas, we will probably fail. Where egos get involved, the light we had is transformed into heat, and the whole effort disintegrates. Thinking stops where anger begins.

It was said of Jesus,

A bruised reed he will not break,
and a smoldering wick he will not snuff out,
till he leads justice to victory.[9]

What an example of the power of benign change!

THREE DESIRED RESPONSES

In the course of this book we have explored a great number of variables that demand consideration as we move into the future as God's people. Many of these are in tension—even paradoxical to one another. For example, we need to hold to our heritage while pioneering new forms of ministry, to preserve our traditions while being free from their control. We must adapt to unbelievers without taking on their beliefs or values and maintain unity while encouraging diversity. In short, we must change while not changing!

How do we bake a cake with such a recipe? Obviously all of these ingredients cannot be blended into a single mix. There are three possible approaches to implementing these things. I trust the reader will find himself or herself identifying with one of the three. The right one will come clear, I trust, as he or she prayerfully weighs the options and consults with others in his or her community of believers. Circumstances, opportunities, and sense of calling, as we saw in 1 Corinthians 7, also serve to guide us at a time like this.

Major Inner Change, Minor Visible Change

James the brother of Jesus is one of my Bible heroes. He epitomized the things we have said about the freedom and liberty that is ours in Christ. His vision was broad enough to embrace the world, but he never left Jerusalem. He chose to exercise his freedom by giving his life to serving a body of believers that was a subculture within a subculture.

As we saw in chapter 7, it was James who finally settled the debate recorded in Acts 15 in which the Jewish believers were insisting that Gentiles had to abide by the laws of Moses. He settled it with his insightful application of the prophecies of Amos to the immediate situation. Thus James led the way in providing space for the Gentiles in God's family. He probably would have excelled in working among Gentiles had his calling taken him in that direction. But he, together with Peter and John, understood that they were called to work with the Jews. Years later, in Acts 21, we find James still in Jerusalem, faithfully leading the church in that city. Even at that juncture the Jewish believers remained adamant about the importance of the Mosaic Law. The amazing thing about James is that this man, who had a vision for a global gospel, was able to minister among a people who were never able to embrace that vision. To the end they were people who, because of their deeply ingrained religious and cultural traditions, could never get beyond the idea that circumcision and the Mosaic Law were essential to godliness.

James chose to exercise his freedom by serving people who were extremely limited in their own freedom. He chose to accept their limitations, to not make an issue of them, for the sake of the great harvest their fellow Jews represented and for the sake of bringing those who came to faith to live in a way that brought glory to God.

James was the ultimate free man. Most of us pursue freedom in order to have the space to be different. James used his freedom to serve people who needed to remain the same. They were people who could not imagine living outside the confines of their own traditions. As such, he is a model for a possible response a reader might have to this book.

Wisdom is knowing when change would be constructive, and when it would be destructive. If change would destroy the *sense of place* of a group of believers, it might be better to not change at all—externally. But here we need to take a lesson from James.

Externally he was as traditional as Moses. Internally he was as free as the Apostle Paul. We can work at preserving the continuity of our churches, and at the same time have a vision for all we have talked about in this book. We must do this. We must preserve the good in what is there, but we must also think beyond what is there—to what needs to be. At the least, we must permit and accept differences, not insist on conformity.

This response will be signaled by affirming the need for the new initiatives along the lines we have been describing. This affirmation will express itself by encouraging, defending, and supporting the new multiform expressions of God's people that need to appear.

Be a People Sown in the World

Priscilla and Aquila modeled this response. They were a Jewish couple originally from Pontus who were driven out of their home when the emperor, Claudius, expelled all Jews from Rome. They were tradespeople who made tents. The Bible doesn't record all their movements, but when we first learn of them they were in Corinth, working their trade and ministering to people. For reasons the Bible doesn't explain, their stay in Corinth was temporary. When we next hear of them they are in an unnamed city in Asia—and they have a church in their home.[10]

It was persecution that moved Priscilla and Aquila out into the world. That wasn't the first time persecution served the purpose of getting God's people to infiltrate by scattering, nor was it the last by any means. Wisdom would instruct us to volunteer to be scattered!

This second possible response by a community of believers would be expressed by giving priority to the local expansion of the gospel. It would probably only be viable to bodies of believers that are still in formation, that have not yet committed themselves to a more traditional set of forms. Some of the implications of this response would be as follows:

◆ The emphasis on enabling people to minister among unbelievers would at least equal that on gathering for worship and teaching.

♦ A corresponding division of human and financial resources.

♦ Appropriately gifted and experienced leadership would be provided—people who can lead others into this ministry by their own example, by what they themselves are doing among unbelievers.

♦ The agenda of such a fellowship would reflect this commitment to scattering. The scheduling of the few centralized functions would not compete for the scarce prime times in the week when unbelievers are available to interact on serious matters.

♦ The focal point of such a community would be those people out there manning their *small boats*. They would be supported by prayer, opportunities for mutual encouragement, teaching and coaching, and a timely helping hand when needed.

Such a community of believers will reflect this in virtually every area of practice. It will be expressed in the kind of people they choose as their leaders, in what they judge to be success and growth, in the kind of facilities they need, and in how they spend their money.

There is probably a middle ground between the first and second response. A body of believers that employs the familiar forms can, at the same time, conceivably release those in its fellowship who feel their calling is to the lost. But for this to work, the body and its leaders would have to exercise unusual restraint and not impose the conventional expectations for attendance, etc., by either those who go, or by those who come to Christ through their efforts.

Recover the Apostolic Team

Several years ago my wife and I visited a newlywed couple in a neighboring city. They had been Christians for about a year and had been married for a month. In a sense, they were spiritual orphans, as the people who had started them in their walk with God had moved away. In the course of our day together, Oscar observed, "We have been married for a month already, but we have not yet had any of our unbelieving friends over for a meal.

There's no excuse for that." That comment caught my attention, and we began to give Oscar and Cristina the help they needed to grow and to minister.

In a matter of a few months, the couple was surrounded by friends who were discovering Christ through their witness. The next thing we knew, Oscar was traveling to a city several hours away to initiate the same process with his brother and his circle of friends. Then, when another new believer had to move to a neighboring city because of a job transfer, Oscar seized the opportunity to make a new planting in that place as well. Oscar thinks like an apostle.

Few people have that mind-set, but those who do can be easily recognized. They are initiators, doers, who think strategically about one thing—the expansion of the gospel! They are frontline people more than they are overseers or managers. They do it themselves. They win the lost, nurture those they win, and stay at it until what they have started is far enough along to thrive on its own. Recently I met a person who was on a team that planted a church without leading anyone to Christ in the process. That is not what I'm talking about. The apostolic team works with unbelievers as its raw material.

In chapter 4 we observed that the people of God need the full spectrum of functions described in Ephesians 4:11: apostles, prophets, evangelists, pastors, and teachers. The apostolic team needs to bring, or rapidly develop, these functions if the body they establish is to be complete. This does not imply a four- or five-person team as it might appear. Often two well-matched couples can embody all these functions.

The people involved in apostolic efforts in the first century were a small fraction of the whole of God's people. It didn't take many then, and it will take comparatively few today to accomplish what needs to be done. But they will need the spiritual and material support from others in the body. And they will need freedom to go and respond to those they seek to reach according to their needs. There is a strong temptation for those who do the sending to attempt to control efforts of those who go. When that happens, the integrity of the effort is inevitably compromised. As James the elder said, "We should not make it difficult for the Gentiles who are turning to God."[11]

A FINAL MESSAGE TO OUR LEADERS

With the biblical foundations of our culture eroding, the believing community finds itself increasingly affected. We are in trouble. This places a great responsibility upon the leaders of our churches. They can maintain the status quo, or they can lead us back to doing "the things [we] did at first."[12]

Recall the thesis of this book:

- ◆ God's people are in the world to bear witness to the world. They are to live among unbelievers, serving them, revealing Christ to them.
- ◆ Ministry depends upon every believer. We are all to use whatever we have to serve God by serving one another and our neighbors.

If this thesis is indeed central to the function of God's people, it will serve as a guiding light to firmer ground for us. It will be a major part of our response to the threat of pluralism and related philosophies. Truth is to be lived. Jesus said, "Now that you know these things, you will be blessed if you do them."[13] It takes experience to transform true information into true conviction. Christians who are primarily spectators, or whose service has not gotten beyond helping with the chores around the home church, have little demand for putting truth to the test. This leaves them especially vulnerable to the prevailing winds of philosophy that are blowing across the nation.

The Apostle Paul wrote to Philemon, "I pray that you may be active in sharing your faith, so that you will have a full understanding of every good thing we have in Christ."[14] Paul's first concern was Philemon himself. He knew Philemon's intimacy with Christ; the depth of that relationship depended in part upon his sharing what he did know about Christ.

A common tendency among us today is to remain unengaged, uncommitted to other people. Life is already too busy, too hectic, so it is easier to rely on and support a pastoral staff and stay in the bleachers. To correct this is the leadership challenge of the day. If our leaders cater to this weakness, we will continue to turn inward, serving ourselves and increasing our isolation from the unbelievers around us. But if they lead, equip, and empower us, we can fulfill God's purpose for our presence in the world.

Notes

▼

Preface
1. See Matthew 4:23, 9:35.
2. Matthew 24:14.
3. See Acts 20:25, 28:23.
4. Matthew 16:18.

**Chapter One—The Reshaping
of the American Way of Life**
1. Joel A. Barker, *Discovering the Future* (Lake Elmo, MN: I.L.I. Press, 1989), page 60.
2. Bill Garrison, "A Theology of the Laity" (unpublished paper for presentation and discussion at the "Lausanne II Conference" in the Philippines, July 1989), page 8.
3. Remarks made at the "Consultation on the Christian Church Under Persecution," Fieldstead Institute (Glen Eyrie, CO, September 10-14, 1989).
4. Allan Bloom, *The Closing of the American Mind* (New York: Simon and Schuster, 1987), page 25.
5. Robert N. Bellah, *Habits of the Heart* (New York: Harper and Row, 1985), page 6.

6. Peter G. Peterson, "The Morning After," *The Atlantic Monthly* (October 1987), page 60.

7. Susan Littwin, *The Postponed Generation* (New York: William Morrow, 1986), page 37.

8. Nancy Gibbs, "How America Has Run Out of Time," *Time*, April 24, 1989, page 60.

9. Gibbs, page 58.

10. Paul Taylor, "Panelists Urge Greater Funding of Measures to Reinforce Family," *Minneapolis Star Tribune*, Tuesday, April 23, 1991, pages 1E-2E.

11. Wanda Urbanska, *The Singular Generation* (Garden City, NY: Doubleday, 1986), pages 1-3.

12. Littwin, page 29.

13. Littwin, page 25.

14. Mack as quoted in Littwin, page 24.

15. Barbara Whitehead as quoted in Taylor, page 2E.

16. John 17:18.

Chapter Two—Our Contemporary Society:
Where We Got It and Where It Is Going

1. Kenneth Scott Latourette, *Beginnings to 1500*, vol. 1 of *A History of Christianity* (New York: Harper and Row, 1975), page 97.

2. Paul Johnson, *A History of Christianity* (Atheneum, NY: Macmillan, 1976), page 116.

3. Johnson, page 120.

4. Johnson, pages 219-220.

5. Johnson, page 206.

6. Johnson, page 328.

7. Johnson, page 336.

8. Johnson, page 353.

9. Johnson, page 350.

10. Allan Bloom, *The Closing of the American Mind* (New York: Simon and Schuster, 1987), pages 168-196.

11. Paul Johnson, *Modern Times* (New York: Harper and Row, 1983), pages 1-8.

12. Johnson, *Modern Times*, page 4.

13. James Hitchcock, *What Is Secular Humanism?* (Ann Arbor, MI: Servant Books, 1982), page 45.

14. Johnson, *Modern Times*, page 10.
15. Johnson, *A History of Christianity*, pages 483, 484.
16. Johnson, pages 485-486.
17. Os Guinness, "Mission in the Face of Modernity," *World Evangelization*, November-December 1989/January 1990, page 11.
18. Guinness, page 11.
19. Guinness, page 10.
20. See Russell Chandler, *Understanding the New Age* (Waco, TX: Word, 1988).
21. Romans 1:32.
22. Isaiah 34:2, Amos 2:6-8, Jeremiah 18:7-10.

Chapter Three—God's People in Society: Why Are We Here?

1. See Genesis 3:21-24.
2. 1 Corinthians 15:50.
3. John 1:29.
4. 2 Corinthians 5:18; see also verses 17-21.
5. Luke 19:10.
6. Mark 2:16-17.
7. Luke 15:7.
8. Matthew 24:14.
9. Matthew 28:19.
10. Mark 16:15.
11. Luke 24:47.
12. John 17:15-21.
13. Isaiah 43:6-7.
14. Ephesians 1:12.
15. John 1:14, NIV, 2nd ed. (Grand Rapids, MI: Zondervan Publishing House, 1978).
16. John 11:4 (emphasis added).
17. See John 12:23.
18. John 13:31.
19. 1 John 3:16.
20. John 16:14.
21. John 17:1.
22. John 17:3.
23. John 21:19 (emphasis added).

24. 1 Peter 1:6.
25. Romans 8:17-18.
26. Revelation 6:10-11.
27. John 18:37.
28. Luke 23:47.
29. Josef Tson, lecture given at the "Consultation on the Christian Church Under Persecution," Fieldsted Institute (Glen Eyrie, CO, September 10-14, 1989).
30. Ephesians 3:10.
31. Matthew 5:16 (RSV, emphasis added).
32. 1 Peter 2:12 (emphasis added).
33. John 17:15,18.
34. Matthew 13:24-30.
35. Matthew 13:38-39.
36. Mark 4:26-28.
37. John 12:23-26.
38. John 12:26.
39. Matthew 20:28.
40. Mark 9:35.
41. 1 Peter 4:10.
42. Ephesians 4:12.
43. Kenneth Scott Latourette, *Beginnings to 1500*, vol. 1 of *A History of Christianity* (New York: Harper and Row, 1975), page 106.
44. F. F. Bruce, *The Spreading Flame* (Grand Rapids, MI: The Paternoster Press, Eerdmans, 1958), pages 190, 191.
45. James 1:27.
46. John 1:14 (NIV, 2nd ed.).
47. 1 Thessalonians 1:5.
48. 1 Corinthians 15:31.
49. Ephesians 4:16.
50. 1 Peter 4:10.
51. 1 Corinthians 7:17.
52. Isaiah 60:22.

Part II—From Acts to the Present: An Historical Review
1. Matthew 22:40.
2. Luke 10:29.

Chapter Four—How Did the Gospel Grow?
An Historical Look at the New Testament

1. Acts 2:5.
2. Acts 2:22.
3. Acts 5:13-14.
4. Acts 6:13-14.
5. Acts 7:49.
6. John 4:23.
7. Acts 11:19.
8. Acts 1:6.
9. Acts 13:1.
10. Acts 20:27.
11. See Acts 20:4, Titus 1:5, 1 Corinthians 4:16-17.
12. Romans 15:20,23.
13. 2 Corinthians 10:13-16.
14. Philippians 2:14-16.
15. Acts 10:28.
16. Paul Johnson, *A History of Christianity* (Atheneum, NY: Macmillan, 1976), page 36.
17. Johnson, page 36.
18. Ephesians 3:3.
19. Galatians 1:11-12.
20. Ephesians 3:5.
21. Ephesians 3:6.
22. See 1 Corinthians 9:19-23.
23. See Acts 14:1-4,14; Romans 16:7; 1 Corinthians 3:21-22; 4:6,9; 2 Corinthians 11:13; Philippians 2:25; 1 Thessalonians 1:1; 2:6-7; Revelation 2:2.
24. See Gerhard Kittel, et al., *Theological Dictionary of the New Testament* (Grand Rapids, MI: Eerdmans, 1976), pages 398-429.
25. Ephesians 4:11-12.
26. Ephesians 4:16.
27. 2 Corinthians 11:2.
28. Ephesians 5:8-16.
29. Kenneth Scott Latourette, *Beginnings to 1500*, vol. 1 of *A History of Christianity* (New York: Harper and Row, 1975), pages 117-118.

Chapter Five—From Ignatius to the Puritans: AD 95-1620

1. Will and Ariel Durant, *The Lessons of History* (New York: Simon and Schuster, 1968), page 12.
2. Michael Green, *Evangelism in the Early Church* (Grand Rapids, MI: Eerdmans, 1970).
3. Paul Johnson, *A History of Christianity* (Atheneum, NY: Macmillan, 1976), page 45.
4. Johnson, page 52.
5. Johnson, page 53.
6. 1 John 1:1-3.
7. 1 John 4:2.
8. Johnson, page 56.
9. Ignatius, *The Epistle of Ignatius to the Smyrnaeans I*, as quoted by Earl D. Radmacher, *What the Church Is All About* (Chicago, IL: Moody Press, 1972), page 36.
10. Irenaeus: *Against Heresies* 3:3:1-2, as quoted by Radmacher, pages 39-40.
11. David J. Bosch, *Transforming Mission* (Maryknoll, NY: Orbis Books, 1991), page 53.
12. Cyprian, as quoted by Radmacher, page 42.
13. Cyprian, as quoted by Radmacher, page 43.
14. Cyprian, as quoted by Radmacher, page 43.
15. Johnson, page 56 (emphasis added).
16. Kenneth Scott Latourette, *Beginnings to 1500*, vol. 1 of *A History of Christianity* (New York: Harper and Row, 1975), page 176.
17. Latourette, page 262.
18. Johnson, page 115.
19. Johnson, pages 115-116.
20. F. F. Bruce, *The Spreading Flame* (Grand Rapids, MI: The Paternoster Press, Eerdmans, 1958), pages 333-339.
21. Matthew 24:9-11.
22. John 17:11-18.
23. Acts 1:4-5.
24. Acts 20:32.
25. Johnson, page 76.
26. Johnson, pages 132-136.
27. Johnson, page 199.

28. Johnson, page 197.
29. Latourette, *Beginnings to 1500*, page 664.
30. Latourette, page 678.
31. Kenneth Scott Latourette, *A.D. 1500–A.D. 1975*, vol. 2 of *A History of Christianity* (New York: Harper and Row, 1975), page 717.
32. Martin Luther, "The Papacy at Rome," in *The Works of Martin Luther*, as quoted by Radmacher, pages 59-60.
33. Luther, as quoted by Radmacher, page 61.
34. Latourette, page 756.
35. Henry Bettenson, *Documents of the Christian Church* (New York: Oxford University Press, 1947), pages 321, 323.
36. Robert N. Bellah, *Habits of the Heart* (New York: Harper and Row, 1985), page 220.
37. Peter Marshall and David Manuel, *The Light and the Glory* (Old Tappan, NJ: Revell, 1977), page 173.
38. Marshall and Manuel, page 187

Chapter Six—The Church in America

1. Howard Snyder, *The Community of the King* (Downers Grove, IL: InterVarsity Press, 1977), page 95.
2. George Barna, *Marketing the Church* (Colorado Springs, CO: NavPress, 1988), page 23.
3. Leith Anderson, *Dying for Change* (Minneapolis, MN: Bethany House, 1990), page 51.
4. Peter F. Drucker, "Marketing 101 for a Fast-Changing Decade," *Wall Street Journal*, November 20, 1990.
5. Anderson, page 50.
6. Anderson, page 27.
7. Richard C. Halverson, *Perspective*, vol. 43, no. 9, April 24, 1991.
8. 1 Corinthians 12:26.
9. Philippians 2:3.
10. Lyle Schaller as quoted by Thomas A. Stewart in "Turning Around the Lord's Business," *Fortune*, September 25, 1989, page 124.
11. Robert E. Slocum, *Maximize Your Ministry* (Colorado Springs, CO: NavPress, 1990), page 70.

12. Slocum, page 55.
13. Jerry Cook, *Love, Acceptance & Forgiveness* (Ventura, CA: Regal, 1979), page 25.
14. Cook, page 39.
15. Stewart, page 116.

Chapter Seven—Freedom and Diversity: A First-Century Example

1. Acts 11:19.
2. Acts 10:2.
3. Acts 10:34-35.
4. Acts 10:45.
5. Acts 11:23.
6. Acts 9:15.
7. Galatians 1:6-7,9.
8. Galatians 2:11-12.
9. See Galatians 2:14, 4:12, 5:2.
10. Galatians 5:2.
11. Acts 15:1.
12. Galatians 2:15.
13. Genesis 17:13.
14. Acts 15:8-9.
15. Acts 15:10.
16. Acts 15:19.
17. Galatians 5:2.
18. Acts 16:3.
19. Acts 21:19-20.
20. Acts 21:21-22.
21. See 1 Corinthians 10:27-33.
22. 1 Corinthians 9:20-21.
23. Galatians 2:2.
24. Galatians 2:7.
25. Galatians 2:9.
26. Galatians 3:22.
27. Galatians 4:3 (emphasis added).
28. Colossians 2:20-23.
29. Galatians 5:1.

30. Galatians 5:13.
31. 1 Corinthians 9:22.

Chapter Eight—To Freedom and Diversity

1. Job 40:15-16,20.
2. Job 41:1,5,33-34.
3. Revelation 5:9.
4. John 8:36.
5. Galatians 5:1.
6. Galatians 5:13.
7. Colossians 1:6 (emphasis added).
8. Acts 15:9, paraphrased.
9. Jaroslav Pelikan as cited by Robert N. Bellah, *Habits of the Heart* (New York: Harper and Row, 1985), page 140.
10. Exodus 18:14.
11. Matthew 23:2-3.
12. John 11:48.
13. Amos 2:4.
14. Ezekiel 20:13.
15. Ezra 7:8,10.
16. Nehemiah 8:3,8.
17. Mark 7:7-8,13.
18. Mark 7:9.
19. John 5:39-40.
20. John 5:45-46.
21. Matthew 23:4,13.
22. Acts 10:28.
23. Acts 11:3.
24. Acts 15:19.
25. Colossians 2:8,20,23.
26. Hebrews 5:14.
27. 2 Kings 18:4.
28. Aleksandr I. Solzhenitsyn, *The Oak and the Calf* (New York: Harper and Row, 1975), page 303.

Chapter Nine—New Boundaries for the Church

1. 2 Timothy 3:16-17.
2. 1 Corinthians 8:2.

3. See Psalm 19:1-4.
4. See Ezekiel 11:10.
5. See Hebrews 1:1.
6. See Romans 9:11-18.
7. See Romans 10:14.
8. See John 16:8.
9. See 1 Peter 2:9.
10. 1 Corinthians 12:4-6.
11. 1 Corinthians 12:25.
12. See Romans 12:3-21, 1 Corinthians 12, Ephesians 4:1-16, 1 Peter 4:7-11.
13. Ephesians 4:15-16.
14. 1 Corinthians 12:11.
15. 1 Corinthians 2:16.
16. 2 Corinthians 1:24.
17. See 1 John 1:7.
18. See Ephesians 5:8-16.
19. 1 Peter 4:8.
20. Romans 12:16.
21. Galatians 6:10.
22. Hebrews 13:3.
23. Ephesians 4:11-12.
24. Donald McGilchrist, "Leadership in a Centered-Set Model" (unpublished paper, October 1989), page 3.
25. Ephesians 5:21.
26. Ephesians 4:16.
27. Hebrews 13:17.

Chapter Ten—God's People
in the Midst of Postmodern America

1. Allan Bloom, *The Closing of the American Mind* (New York: Simon and Schuster, 1987), page 58.
2. Camille Paglia, "She Wants Her TV! He Wants His Book!" *Harper's Magazine*, March 1991, pages 47, 48-49, 50, 54.
3. Bloom, page 34.
4. Robert N. Bellah, *Habits of the Heart* (New York: Harper and Row, 1985), page 76.
5. George Gallup as cited by Tom Morton, "Americans Called

Religious Hypocrites," *Gazette Telegraph,* May 10, 1990.

6. Morton.

7. Gallup as cited by A. H. M., "Gallup Tells Editors: Americans Revere the Bible, Don't Read It," *World* (formerly *Presbyterian Journal*), May 19, 1990.

8. George Barna and William McKay, *Vital Signs: Emerging Social Trends and the Future of American Christianity* (Westchester, IL: Crossway, 1984), page 136.

9. Kenneth Woodward, et al., "A Time to Seek," *Newsweek,* December 17, 1990, page 56.

10. Matthew 5:13.

Chapter Eleven—The Task Before Us

1. Lesslie Newbigin, *The Gospel in a Pluralist Society* (Grand Rapids, MI: Eerdmans, 1989), page 7.

2. John 14:6.

3. 1 Corinthians 2:2,4.

4. E. Stanley Jones, *A Song of Ascents* (Nashville, TN: Abingdon, 1968), page 86.

5. Jones, page 91.

6. Jones, page 107.

7. Newbigin, page 12.

8. 2 Corinthians 4:4.

9. 2 Corinthians 10:3-4.

10. See Ephesians 6:18, Hebrews 4:12, 1 John 4:12.

11. John 1:14, NIV, 2nd ed. (Grand Rapids, MI: Zondervan Publishing House, 1978) (emphasis added).

12. 1 Thessalonians 1:5 (emphasis added).

13. Ephesians 5:8,14-15 (emphasis added).

14. John 4:38.

15. 1 Corinthians 9:22.

16. 1 Corinthians 10:27.

17. John 17:23.

18. John 20:31.

19. Matthew 9:12-13.

20. John 8:34.

21. Exodus 34:7.

22. Robert N. Bellah, *Habits of the Heart* (New York: Harper and

Row, 1985), page 99.

23. 1 Corinthians 6:9-11 (emphasis added).
24. Corinthians 1:8-9.
25. Romans 5:3.
26. Psalm 119:105.
27. John 3:20-21.
28. Bellah, page 82.
29. James 1:25.
30. James 1:23-24.
31. James 1:21.
32. Psalms 32:3-5.
33. Isaiah 66:2.
34. Galatians 5:22.
35. Philippians 2:13.
36. John 8:34,36.
37. 2 Timothy 1:7 (emphasis added).
38. Dietrich Bonhoeffer, *Life Together* (New York: Harper and Row, 1954), pages 110, 112.

Chapter Twelve—Recovering Our Mobility

1. Galatians 2:1-2,6.
2. Matthew 13:19.
3. 1 Thessalonians 1:5.
4. 1 Thessalonians 1:9.
5. 1 Thessalonians 2:11-12.
6. 1 Thessalonians 1:8.
7. Philippians 2:16.
8. Matthew 15:13.
9. Matthew 12:20.
10. Acts 18:1-2, 1 Corinthians 16:19, 2 Timothy 4:19.
11. Acts 15:19.
12. Revelation 2:5.
13. John 13:17.
14. Philemon 6.

Author

▼

J im Petersen is part of the Resident International Team that oversees the global work of The Navigators, and one of three international vice presidents.

In 1963 Jim pioneered the Navigator ministry in Brazil. He worked among the young educated who were mostly Marxist, agnostic, and hostile toward religion and the institutional Church. Jim's first challenge was to find a way to make Christ understandable to them. The second challenge was to help these new believers create community that would both encourage transformation in every aspect of their lives and keep them involved with their unbelieving friends. Innovative forms and methods had to be devised at every step.

By 1973 the foundations in Brazil were laid and other people, including nationals, were building on them. Jim turned to other Latin American countries, recruiting missionary teams and serving as their "player-coach."

In 1981 believers in Eastern Europe and the Middle East invited Jim to help them learn how to communicate Christ to their neighbors and set up healthy communities.

In 1985 Jim moved to Colorado Springs to be better positioned to serve as an international consultant. His first two books,

Evangelism as a Lifestyle and *Evangelism for Our Generation*, have been integrated into one volume entitled *Living Proof* (1989). This material is also available as a video training course.

Jim and his wife, Marge, have raised four children. They now reside in Colorado Springs, Colorado.